Pearl

BUYING GU

D0444218

Pearl

BUYING GUIDE

Fourth Edition

How to evaluate, identify and select pearls & pearl jewelry

Renée Newman

International Jewelry Publications
Los Angeles _____

Copyright © 2005 by **International Jewelry Publications**

First published 1992
Second Edition 1994
Reprinted 1996
Third Edition 1999
Reprinted 2001
Fourth Edition 2004
Revised 2005

All rights reserved. No part of this book may be used, reproduced, or transmitted in any manner whatsoever without
written permission from the publisher except in the case of
brief quotations used in critical reviews and articles.

   This publication is designed to provide information in
regard to the subject matter covered. It is sold with the un-
derstanding that the publisher and author are not engaged in
rendering legal, financial, or other professional services. If
legal or other expert assistance is required, the services of a
competent professional should be sought. International
Jewelry Publications and the author shall have neither liability
nor responsibility to any person or entity with respect to any
loss or damage caused or alleged to be caused directly or
indirectly by the information contained in this book. All
inquiries should be directed to:

International Jewelry Publications
P.O. Box 13384
Los Angeles, CA 90013-0384 USA

(Inquiries should be accompanied by a self-addressed,
stamped envelope.)

Printed in Singapore

Library of Congress Cataloging-in-Publication Data

Newman, Renée.
    Pearl buying guide: how to evaluate, identify and select
pearls & pearl jewelry / Renée Newman – 4th ed.
        p. cm.
    Includes bibliographical references and index.
    ISBN 0-929975-35-9 (pbk.: alk. paper)
    1. Pearls--Purchasing. I. Title.

TS755.P3N495 2004
639'.412–dc22
                                        2003064037

Cover photos: South Sea Pearls from King Plutarco Inc.,
photography by Richard Rubins.

Photo facing title page: Akoya pearls & photo from Hikari South
Sea Pearl Co.

Title page photo: Mabe pearl earrings by Krespi & White,
photography by Marty Kelly.

Contents

Acknowledgments

I would like to express my appreciation to the following people for their contribution to the *Pearl Buying Guide*:

Ernie and Regina Goldberger of the Josam Diamond Trading Corporation. This book could never have been written without the experience and knowledge I gained from working with them. Some of the pearls pictured in this book are or were part of their collection.

Eve Alfillé, Francisco Adame, Albert Asher, KC. Bell, Charles Carmona, Pin P. Chen, Shane Elan, Patricia Esparza, Susan B. Johnson, Betty Sue King, Chien Lin, Peter Malnekoff, Henri Masliah, Rick Matsui, Lynn Marie Nakamura, Wes Rankin, Avi Raz, Jet Taylor and Charles Ueng. They have made valuable suggestions, corrections and comments regarding the portions of the book they examined. They are not responsible for any possible errors, nor do they necessarily endorse the material contained in this book.

A & Z Pearls, Inc., Adachi America, Inc., Albert Cohen Co., Blue River Gems & Jewelry Co., Gladys Evans, Jye's International, Inc., King Plutarco, Inc., Overland Gems, Inc., Shima Pearl Company, Inc., Timeless Gem Designs, Marge Vaughn, and Yokoo Pearls. Their pearls or clasps have been used for some of the photographs.

Albert Asher South Sea Pearl Co., Eve J. Alfillé Gallery, American Pearl Co, Assael International Inc., K. C. Bell Natural Pearls, Angela Conty, Erica Courtney, Gary Dulac, Divina Pearls, Gemological Institute of America, Hikari South Sea Pearl Co, Inc, Cultured Pearl Association of America, Inter World Trading, Mikimoto (America) Co. Inc, Japan Pearl Exporters' Association, Sandy Jones, King Plutarco, Ponthieux's Jewelry Design, Linda K. Quinn Designs, King's Ransom, Krespi & White, Pacific Coast Pearls, Pearce Design, Mark Schneider Design, Shogun Pearl Co, and Mikhail Smolkin . Photos or diagrams from them have been reproduced in this book.

Gladys Chong, Ion Itescu, Maria Johnson, Dawn King, Donald Nelson, Joyce Ng, Coco Puye, and Monique Truchet. They have provided technical assistance.

Louise Harris Berlin, editor of the *Pearl Buying Guide*. Thanks to her, this book is much easier for consumers to read and understand.

My sincere thanks to all of these contributors for their kindness and help.

1

Pearl Price Factors in a Nutshell

The following factors can affect the price of pearls:
Luster
Surface quality
Shape
Color
Size
Nacre (pearl coating) thickness and quality
Matching
Treatment status (untreated or treated? type of treatment)
Pearl type (saltwater/freshwater, natural/cultured, whole/blister)

LUSTER: Pearl brilliance; the shine and glow of a pearl. The greater and deeper the luster, the more valuable the pearl. Pearls with a high luster display strong and sharp light reflections and a good contrast between the bright and darker areas of the pearl. Pearls with low luster look milky, chalky and dull. Select pearls that have a good luster. For more information, see Chapter 4.

SURFACE QUALITY: The fewer and smaller the flaws, the more valuable the pearl. Blemishes on single pearls tend to be more obvious and less acceptable than those on strands. It's normal for pearl strands to have some flaws. Additional photos and details are provided in Chapter 6.

Natural pearls normally have more flaws than cultured Japanese Akoya pearls. That's because they've been in the oyster longer and have had more time to develop blemishes. Cultured pearls from the South Seas are also more likely to have flaws than Akoyas, which have a thinner nacre coating.

SHAPE: Normally, the more round and symmetrical the pearl, the more it costs. Unique, asymmetrical shapes, however, are also desirable, and are used to create distinctive pearl pieces. The lowest priced shapes are baroque (irregular and asymmetrical in shape) or have ring-like formations encircling the pearl. Chapters 3, 9, 10 and 11 show a wide variety of pearl shapes.

COLOR: Saltwater pearls that are yellowish usually sell for less than those which are white and light pink. Golden South Sea pearls from Indonesia and the Philippines are an exception and can sell for as much as white South Sea pearls, provided the gold color is intense and natural.

Natural-color black pearls (they're actually gray) can sell for as much as white pearls of the same size and quality, as long as they have overtone colors and are not just plain gray. The overtone colors, which are visible in the light-colored areas of black pearls, may be green, pink, blue or purple.

Pink overtones are desirable on white pearls and are visible in the dark areas of the pearl. Greenish or yellowish overtones tend to reduce the price of white pearls. Occasionally, iridescent rainbow-like colors are visible on pearls. Pearl iridescence is always considered a valuable quality.

Luster qualities ranging from high to very low

Surface qualities ranging from clean to heavily blemished

Some South Sea pearl shapes: round, oval, drop, button, circled drop, baroque

Some Australian South Sea pearl colors

Some Indonesian South Sea pearl colors

Some Tahitian pearl colors

The way in which color affects the pricing of freshwater pearls varies from one dealer to another. Often it has little or no effect. However, when comparing the prices of any pearls, try to compare pearls of the same type and color.

SIZE: Usually the larger the pearl the more it costs. Pricing often depends on availability & demand.

NACRE THICKNESS: Nacre (NAY-ker) thickness is not a price factor for natural pearls because they're nearly all nacre (a pearly substance that mollusks secrete around irritants). However, it's of critical importance in cultured saltwater pearls. See Chapter 4. (**Natural pearls** are formed around an irritant such as a shell particle or parasite that accidentally enters a mollusk. **Cultured pearls** are formed after a human intentionally inserts a shell bead nucleus or a piece of oyster or mussel tissue in a mollusk. If the bead nucleus isn't left in the mollusk long enough, the mollusk won't have time to coat it with enough microscopic layers of nacre to make a lustrous pearl).

The thicker the nacre coating of a pearl, the better and more durable the pearl. South Sea pearls normally have a thicker nacre coating than Akoya pearls. Nacre thickness is one of the most important quality factors for cultured saltwater pearls because it affects both pearl beauty and durability.

Nacre thickness is not as important a factor in cultured freshwater pearls as it is in saltwater pearls. This is because most freshwater pearls have no shell nucleus. When one is present, the nacre is usually thicker than in Akoya pearls. One of the biggest selling points of cultured freshwater pearls is that they usually have a higher percentage of pearl nacre than their saltwater counterparts.

MATCHING: The better pearls blend together in terms of color, shape, luster, size and surface quality, the more valuable they are. Finding well-matched, high quality pearls can be a challenge.

TREATMENT STATUS: Dyed and irradiated pearls cost less than those of natural color. Irradiated pearls normally cost more than dyed pearls because the irradiation process is more costly and because it's usually reserved for higher quality pearls. Other kinds of treatments and tests for detecting dyed pearls are discussed in Chapter 12.

During the 1920's and 30's, however, dyed black pearls were considered fashionable and sometimes sold for as much as white pearls of similar size and quality.

PEARL TYPE: Before you price a pearl, you should know, for example, if it's **saltwater** (from the oceans, sea, gulf or bay) or if it's **freshwater** (from a river, lake or pond). Good saltwater pearls (e.g., South Sea and Japanese Akoya) can cost several times more than freshwater pearls of similar quality and size. One of the reasons for this is that one mussel in a lake can produce as many as forty freshwater pearls in one harvest. An oyster in the sea typically produces one or sometimes two saltwater pearls at a time. It should be noted, however, that some strands of large round pink freshwater pearls have retailed for over $10,000.

Natural pearls are more valuable than cultured pearls. Chapter 14 explains how to distinguish cultured pearls from those that are natural.

Whole pearls are much more valued than **blister pearls**— those which grow attached to the inner surface of a mollusk shell and **three-quarter pearls**—whole pearls that have been ground or sawed on one side, usually to remove blemishes. **Mabe pearls** are made from blister pearls by removing the interior, filling it with a paste and covering it with a mother of pearl backing. These assembled pearls offer a big look at a low price, but they're not as durable as non assembled pearls, which are higher priced. See Chapter 3 for photos and more information.

2

Curious Facts About Pearls

The primary focus of the *Pearl Buying Guide* is the evaluation and identification of pearls. However, it's also helpful to put them in perspective. Below is a brief, unconventional account of the pearl throughout history.

An Apology from the Pearl Family

We pearls want to express our remorse for the suffering we have brought on to pearl oysters and mussels around the world. Unfortunately, many are not around to receive our long overdue apology.

Consider the pearl oysters in Venezuela and Panama, for example. Five-hundred years ago, these oysters were abundant and had a fairly tranquil life in this area. Then Christopher Columbus and Vasco de Balboa arrived and discovered pearls. Until the development of the gold and silver mines in Mexico and Peru, we pearls were the New World's biggest export. In fact, the value of pearls exceeded that of all other exports combined; and in Spain, the Americas became known as "The Lands that Pearls Come From." One of the most famous members of our pearl family, *La Peregrina* ("The Incomparable"), was found in the Americas. A pear-shaped pearl about the size of a pigeon's egg, *La Peregrina* is particularly noted for its beauty. Among its owners have been Philip II of Spain, Mary Tudor of England, Napoleon III and Elizabeth Taylor. According to one story, the slave diver that found it was rewarded with his freedom and his master with a plot of land and a position as mayor.

Nowadays the number of oysters producing pearls around Venezuela and Panama is insignificant. One reminder of what an important source of pearls this area once was is the name of an island off the Venezuelan coast, the Isle of Margarita. "Margarita" means pearls. Incidentally, if your name is Margaret, Peggy, Marjorie, Margot, Maggie, Gretchen, Gretel or Rita, it also means "pearl," which in turn signifies purity, innocence, humility and sweetness.

The overfishing of oysters has not been limited to areas around South and Central America. Pearl oysters and mussels in parts of Europe, North America, and East and West Asia have also either disappeared or been drastically reduced in number.

Besides feeling guilty about the disappearance of so many oysters and mussels, we pearls regret the discomfort we cause to them when they are alive. It might be easier for you to understand what we mean by discomfort if we explained how we originate.

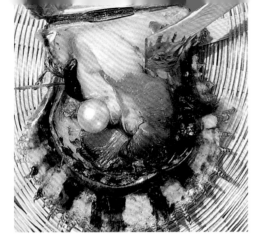

Fig. 2.1 Cultured pearl in a freshly opened oyster. *Photo courtesy of the Japan Pearl Exporter's Association.*

We pearls owe our existence mainly to certain types of saltwater oysters and freshwater mussels. If we are **natural,** then we are usually formed as the mollusk secretes layers of a protective, pearly substance called **nacre** (pronounced NAY-ker) around an irritant. This irritant, which is our **nucleus**, accidentally enters the mollusk and can be a minute snail, worm, fish or crab, or a particle of shell, clay or mud. Experimentation and pearl slicing, however, have led some pearl researchers to believe that most natural round pearls are caused by the accidental entry of a parasitic worm into a mollusk. There aren't many natural pearls produced anymore for them to study. The pearls that are sold today are usually cultured.

If we are **cultured**, then the irritant is intentionally introduced by man. In the case of most freshwater pearls, pieces of mantle (a membranous tissue that secretes nacre and lines the inner shell surface of mollusks) are inserted into a mussel or oyster. Saltwater cultured pearls, however, usually originate from the insertion of a shell bead nucleus along with a bit of oyster mantle tissue into an oyster. In both cases, the shape and size of the resulting pearls depends to a large degree on the shape and size of the implanted irritant.

Sometimes people are surprised to discover how small oysters are for the pearls they host. Japanese pearl oysters grow to only about 10 centimeters (4") in diameter. Imagine what it would be like if you had to carry around a baseball inside of you! This will help you understand why we feel bad about oysters having to put up with us. Besides being a source of irritation, we also lead to their premature death. Many cultured pearl oysters die when a nucleus is inserted or when pearls are later removed.

As we pearls take this occasion to apologize for the miserable fate that we have brought on to the pearl oysters and mussels of this world, we would also like to express our gratitude for their hospitality. Were it not for the oyster and mussel, we pearls would not have the chance to exist.

The Pearl Oysters' Response

We oysters don't harbor any grudges against pearls. They have made our lives worthwhile. Pearls are not responsible for killing off pearl mollusks. Man is. Consider the mussels in Lake Biwa, Japan. They used to be plentiful. Now, due to pollution, the few that are left are struggling to survive.

Consider too the oysters in the Persian Gulf. They used to be renowned for producing the world's finest natural pearls. Overfishing plus the discovery of oil and industrialization of the gulf have disrupted the oyster beds there.

Fig. 2.2 South-Sea Pearl farm in Indonesia. *Photo courtesy Hikari South Sea Pearl Co.*

Left: **Fig 2.3**. Net panel containing oysters with inserted nuclei. Nets are suspended about 3 to 6 meters below the water surface for a cultivation period of about two years.

Below: **Fig 2.4** Insertion of a shell-bead nucleus into a South Sea pearl oyster. *Both photos courtesy Hikari South Sea Pearl Co.*

As for the pearls' concern about irritating us or causing us pain, their worries are exaggerated. Our nervous system is very simple. Consequently, we don't have the same sense of feeling that humans do.

The fame and prestige that pearls have brought to us oysters has more than made up for the minor discomfort they have caused. Maybe you find it hard to understand how something as plain as a pearl could elevate our status. Some background information on it might help explain why.

The pearl is the oldest known gem, and for centuries it was considered the most valuable. To the ancients, pearls were a symbol of the moon and had magical powers which could bring prosperity and long life.

Throughout history, pearls have been considered divine gifts especially suited for royalty. Women who wanted to gain the favor of a king would offer him pearls. In Persia, crowns with double circlets of pearls were the symbol of royal and divine birth. This became a custom elsewhere as well. When Julius Caesar became emperor of the Roman empire, he claimed descent from the gods and was crowned with a pearl diadem.

Pearls, too, have been considered ideal wedding gifts due to their symbolism of purity and innocence. In the Hindu religion, the presentation of an undrilled pearl and its piercing has formed part of the marriage ceremony.

Some cultures, such as the Chinese, have used pearls medically to cure a variety of ailments—indigestion, fever, heart disease. Pearls have also been prescribed as a love potion and tonic for long life. Today, the main component of pearls, calcium carbonate ($CaCO_3$), is used as an antacid and a dietary supplement. Calcium manganese carbonate is an important heart medicine. At the age of 94, Mikimoto, the founder of the cultured pearl industry stated, "I owe my fine health and long life to the two pearls I have swallowed every morning of my life since I was twenty."

The unique qualities of the pearl were particularly well described by George Kunz and Charles Stevenson in 1908 in *The Book of the Pearl* (page 305).

> Unlike other gems, the pearl comes to us perfect and beautiful, direct from the hand of nature. Other precious stones receive careful treatment from the lapidary, and owe much to his art. The pearl, however, owes nothing to man...It is absolutely a gift of nature, on which man cannot improve. We turn from the brilliant, dazzling ornament of diamonds or emeralds to a necklace of pearls with a sense of relief, and the eye rests upon it with quiet, satisfied repose and is delighted with its modest splendor, its soft gleam, borrowed from its home in the depths of the sea. It seems truly to typify steady and abiding affection, which needs no accessory or adornment to make it more attractive. And there is a purity and sweetness about it which makes it especially suitable for the maiden.

Had it not been for the pearl, we oysters would have probably been scorned as lowly, slothful creatures. Instead we're recognized as the creator of an extraordinary gem—one symbolic of all that is pure and beautiful. Therefore we'd like to take this occasion to thank all pearls for the esteem they have brought to our species. We oysters are proud to be their hosts.

3

Pearl Types & Shapes

When you think of a pearl, what's the first shape and color that comes to your mind? Probably round and white. But if you lived in Tahiti, you might initially think of a dark grayish pearl and it wouldn't necessarily be round. Pearls come in a wide range of shapes, types and colors; in this chapter we'll define the various types and explain the role that shape plays in determining the value of a pearl.

Pearl Types

The difference between natural and cultured pearls was explained in Chapter 2. Technically the term **pearl** should only refer to a natural pearl. Nevertheless, cultured pearls are so common now and natural ones so rare that "pearl" normally refers to a cultured pearl (One exception is in certain Arab countries where cultured pearls tend to be frowned upon. Pearls there are generally considered a special gift from God that should be entirely a product of nature.) In this book, for the sake of brevity, cultured pearls will often be labeled as "pearls." When shopping for pearls, you may come across the term **semi-cultured**. It refers to imitation pearls. Many members of the trade consider it a deceptive term designed to trick buyers into thinking they are getting cultured pearls when they aren't.

Pearls can additionally be classed as saltwater or freshwater. People tend to be most familiar with **saltwater pearls**, which come from oysters in oceans, seas, gulfs and bays. The best-known example is the Akoya pearl shown in figure 3.1 and discussed on the next page

Freshwater pearls (fig. 3.3) are found in mussels or oysters in rivers, lakes or ponds and tend to be more irregular in shape and more varied in color than pearls found in saltwater oysters. Chapter 11 provides more information on freshwater pearls.

Pearls are further classified into the categories below:

Oriental Pearls   Natural pearls found in oysters of the Persian Gulf or those that look like pearls found there (according to the USA Federal Trade Commission). Sometimes this term is used to designate either any natural saltwater pearl or else more specifically, any natural saltwater pearl found in the West Asia Area, e.g. in the Red Sea, the Persian Gulf or the Gulf of Mannar off the west coast of Sri Lanka.

A more precise definition of "Oriental pearl" is given by the respected pearl researcher, Koji Wada, in Pearls of the World (pg. 69): "natural pearls from one kind of sea-water pearl oyster called the wing shell."

Fig. 3.1 High quality Japanese Akoya cultured pearls (saltwater pearls) ranging in body color from white to dyed blue and dyed black. *Photo from Hikari South Sea Pearl Co.*

Akoya Pearls

Saltwater pearls from the Akoya oyster (*Pinctada fucata martensii*), which are usually cultured (fig. 3.1). These pearls are typically roundish, and their natural body colors normally range from light pink, to white, to yellowish. The chapters on pearl quality in this book focus on Akoya pearls.

Even though they are often called Japanese pearls, they can also be found in oysters outside Japan. In fact, China has become the major producer of Akoya pearls less than 7 mm in size. Korea, Hong Kong and Sri Lanka are already culturing pearls using the Akoya oyster. Currently, most Akoya pearls over 7 mm are cultured in Japan.

South Sea Pearls

Used sometimes as a general term signifying any saltwater pearl found in the area extending from the Philippines and Indonesia down to Australia and across to French Polynesia (fig 3.4). More often than not, it refers specifically to large white or yellow pearls cultured in the *Pinctada maxima* oyster—a large oyster found in the South Seas, also called the silver-lip or yellow-lip (also gold-lip) oyster depending on the color of its shell lip.

South Sea pearls tend to range from 9–19 mm, whereas Akoya pearls usually range from 1–10 mm. A more detailed discussion of South Sea pearls is found in Chapter 9.

Black Pearls

Pearls of natural color (not dyed) from the black-lip (*Pinctada margaritifera*) oyster in the Western to Central Pacific Ocean or from the La Paz pearl oyster (Pinctada mazatlanica) or rainbow-lipped oyster (*Pteria sterna*) in the Eastern Pacific between Baja California and Peru. Some people use the term "black pearl" to refer to any dark colored pearl, dyed or natural color. (See Chapter 10.)

Biwa Pearls

Freshwater pearls cultivated in Lake Biwa, Japan's largest lake (fig. 3.2). Sometimes other freshwater cultured pearls are called Biwas in order to impress buyers. Lake Biwa was one of the first freshwater culturing sites and it has been noted for its high quality pearls. Because of pollution, production has come to a standstill.

Fig. 3.2 Freshwater Biwa pearl set in 18K gold. *Figurine by A & Z Pearls; photo by Richard Rubins.*

Fig. 3.3 Chinese freshwater pearls

Fig. 3.4 Pearls from the South Seas. *Photo by Ralph Gabriner; necklaces by Erica Courtney .*

Fig. 3.5 Whole black and white South-Sea pearls with an acorn shape. They resemble 3/4 pearls when mounted in this brooch. *Photo and jewelry from Albert Asher South Sea Pearl Co.*

Fig. 3.6 A 3/4 pearl which could look like a whole pearl if mounted in a closed-back setting.

Kasumiga™

Pearls named after Lake Kasumigara, north of Tokyo, where they are cultured in *Hyriopsis schlegelii x Hyriopsis cumingii* hybrid mussels. Kasumiga™ pearls, which have also been generically called Kasumi pearls, were introduced to the market in the mid 1990's and are only available in limited quantities. These nucleated freshwater pearls range in size from 11–16 mm and in color from purple to pink to white to gold. See figure 3.9.

Blue Pearls

Dark-colored pearls found in oysters such as the Akoya or silver-lip oysters. The color is due to foreign contaminants in the nacre or between the nacre and shell bead nucleus unlike black pearls whose color is an inherent characteristic of the pearl nacre. (Hisada and Komatsu, *Pearls of the World*, page 88 and Robert Webster, *Gems*, page 506).

Half Pearls

"Whole pearls that have been ground or sawed on one side, usually to remove blemishes" (as defined in *The GIA Jeweler's Manual*). If the sawed pearl looks too large to be a half pearl, it's called a **three-quarter pearl** (fig. 3.6). Half and three-quarter pearls are priced lower than whole pearls of the same shape and quality. Button- and acorn-shape South-Sea pearls have a flattened side which can make them look like a half or three-quarter pearls when mounted (fig. 3.5).

The term "half pearl" is sometimes used to refer to blister pearls.

Blister Pearls

Natural or cultured pearls that grow attached to the inner surface of the oyster or mussel shell. When cut from the shell, one side is left flat with no pearly coating. (Some people apply the term "blister" only to natural pearls of this type. Cultured blister pearls are not new. As far back as the 13th century, the Chinese were placing small lead images of the sitting Buddha inside freshwater mussels against their shells. The resulting pearly buddhas were either removed and sold as good-luck charms or else left attached to the shell and used as an ornamental curiosity.

Tennessee is a major source of cultured solid blister pearls. These American blister pearls come in a variety of shapes and are marketed under the name of domé® (fig 3.8). Their nacre is thicker than that of mabe pearls, making them more durable.

Fig. 3.7 A selection of South Sea and Akoya mabe pearls from King Plutarco Co.

Mabe Pearls	Assembled cultured blister pearls (fig. 3.7) (pronounced MAH-bay). The blister pearl is cultured by gluing against the inside of the shell a half-bead nucleus (often of plastic or soapstone). After the mollusk has secreted nacre over the bead, the blister pearl is cut from the shell; and the bead is removed so the pearl can be cleaned to prevent deterioration. The remaining hole is filled with a paste or wax (and sometimes also a bead) and then covered with a mother-of-pearl backing. Mabe pearls are not as not as durable as solid blister pearls.

It can be hard to distinguish between mabe, blister or half pearls when they are mounted in jewelry. As a consequence, these three terms often end up being used interchangeably.

Despite all the work involved in assembling mabe pearls, they are relatively inexpensive for their large size. This is partly because several can be grown in one oyster and because they are grown in oysters that have rejected a whole nucleus or that are judged unsuitable for producing whole pearls. Also, any type of half pearl will cost far less than if it were whole, no matter what type of oyster it is grown in.

Most large mabe assembled pearls come from the silver-lip or black-lip oysters, but technically the term "mabe" should only refer to pearls cultivated in mabe oysters (*Pteria penguin*). The true **mabe-oyster pearls** are known for having a better luster, color and iridescence than pearls cultured in other oysters and are, consequently, more valuable. Most of those harvested are ½ or ¾ blister pearls. If a salesperson claims that the jewelry you are buying

19

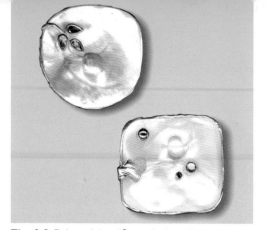

Fig. 3.8 Cultured domé® pearls from Tennessee set with sapphires and tourmalines. *Design copyright, Eve Alfillé; photo by Matthew Arden.*

Fig. 3.9 Lake Kasumigara 13 mm pearl and tourmaline earrings. *Design copyright by Eve Alfillé; photo by Matthew Arden.*

is made with a mabe-oyster pearl, have him or her write this on the receipt. It's helpful for insurance and appraisal purposes. Information on the culturing of mabe oysters can be found in a write-up by Morimitsu Muramatsu in *Pearls of the World* (pp. 79 to 86).

"Mabe Blister Pearls"

An informal term used by some dealers to designate mabe pearls with a rim, making them resemble a fried egg (fig. 3.10). The term "blister mabe" is also used. Technically, though, all assembled mabe pearls originate as blister pearls and after they are assembled, they are mabe pearls with a rim.

"Rainbow pearls"

A trade name for pearls from the Western winged (rainbow-lipped) pearl oyster (*Pteria sterna*), which is noted for its high luster and rainbow-like colors. This oyster ranges naturally off the eastern Pacific Coast from California to Peru. Some are cultivated as mabe and whole pearls near Guaymas, Mexico.

Fig. 3.10 Mabe pearls with a nacre rim— "Blister mabe pearls"

"Rainbow pearls," which are generically called "black pearls," are found in a variety of colors: lavender, pink, red, blue, green, purple, silver, gold, black and brown with varying shades and combinations. It's not unusual to see three or four color variations on one pearl. Whole cultured rainbow pearls range from 7 to about 12 mm in diameter and have a good nacre thickness. Their natural counterparts are found in sizes from seed to 30-carat pearls and range in price from $100 per carat to $2000 per carat wholesale. Cultured rainbow pearls cost less, with mabes being the least expensive.

Fig. 3.11 A 42-strand Akoya keshi necklace. *Photo by John Parrish; necklace from A & Z Pearls.*

Fig. 3.12 Natural rainbow pearls (black pearls from the *Pteria sterna* oyster). *Pearls/photo: Pacific Coast Pearls.*

Fig. 3.13 Tiny Tahitian keshi pearls. *Necklace copyright by Eve J. Alfillé; photo credit: Matthew Arden.*

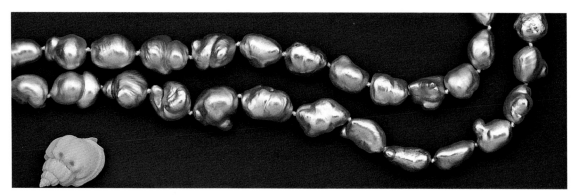

Fig. 3.14 Large Tahitian keshi. *Photo and pearls from Hikari South Sea Pearl Co.*

Seed Pearls   Small, natural pearls which measure about two millimeters or less. They usually weigh less than 0.06 carat.

Keshi   A general term used by pearl traders for pearls that grow accidentally in the soft tissue or the adductor muscle of cultured pearl-bearing mollusks.

Chien Lin, president of Inter World Trading, says that the term "keshi" started out referring to a type of natural pearl in Japan, but over time, the term became much more broadly used internationally. Having grown up in the pearl industry in Kobe, Japan, Lin had the opportunity to meet many old-generation pearl traders. They told him the term "keshi" was initially used to refer to natural seed pearls found when harvesting wild Akoya oysters. Since the tiny natural pearls resembled poppy seeds, they called them *keshi*, which means "poppy" in Japanese. Lin has verified this usage of the term with a specialist at the Mikimoto Pearl Museum in Japan.

After the Japanese started culturing Akoya pearls, the term "keshi" was also used for the by-products of Akoya cultivation that did not contain a bead nucleus. These form from nacre secretion around microorganisms or shell particles that enter the pearl during pearl nucleation. The nacre may also be secreted around detached fragments of the mantle inserted with the pearl nuclei (mantle is a membranous tissue that secretes nacre and lines the inner shell surface of mollusks. It's inserted with the pearl bead nucleus to help stimulate nacre formation). Mantle tissue keshi have also been called "saibo (tissue) keshi," but most traders just call them keshi. Akoya keshi pearls can range from small "seed-sized" to skinny pearls as long as 14 mm.

The term became more confusing when freshwater pearls and South Sea pearls from the silver- and black-lipped oysters entered the market. Keshi from South Sea pearl oysters are generally much larger in size than Akoya pearls because of the size of the mother of pearl and speed of the nacre formation. Even though South Sea keshi seldom look like poppy seeds or tiny pearls, the term "keshi" is used to refer to these by-products of South Sea oysters. There is a large range of sizes for South Sea keshi—from small seed-sized to the size of a baby's fist.

To add another element of confusion to the term "keshi," Chinese reborn freshwater pearls (*Zai Sheng Zhu* in Mandarin) came into the picture. A reborn pearl is grown out of the pearl sack of a mussel in which a pearl was carefully removed at harvest so as to not kill the mussel. Another pearl will grow out of a pearl sack, after healing, without another implantation of a mantle or tissue. (This tissue is originally necessary to initiate the virgin grafting to stimulate pearl nacre formation). Some people call these "born again" pearls.

Freshwater reborn pearls are not new to the market. This category of pearls had been available from Biwa Lake pearl farms in Japan when Biwa pearls were still in production. (Actual pearl cultivation in Biwa Lake faded out in the late 1980's, leaving very few farmers still cultivating on a small scale). At that time, Biwa pearl traders did not use the term "keshi" for reborn pearls; they simply called them "Biwa pearls," the general term for freshwater pearls produced at Biwa Lake.

Some traders refer to Chinese reborn pearls as "natural pearls" or "Biwa pearls," but both terms are wrongfully used. Reborn pearls are not natural pearls because they are cultivated, and "Biwa pearl" is a general term for freshwater

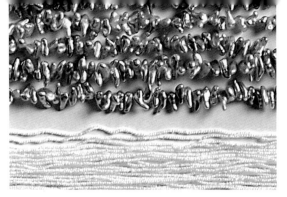

Fig. 3.15 Size ranges of Akoya keshi (actual size). *Pearls and photo from Inter World Trading.*

Fig. 3.16 Freshwater keshi (bottom) and "reborn pearls" (top), actual size. *From Inter World Trading.*

pearls out of Biwa Lake in Japan. Most of the Chinese freshwater pearl cultivation techniques came from Japanese pearl farmers, so too the South Sea pearl cultivation techniques of the black- and silver/gold-lipped pearl oysters.

Chien Lin prefers to refer to these reborn pearls as "keshi-type cultured freshwater pearls" because the nature of the reborn pearls is different from that of other keshi pearls. Reborn pearls are intentionally created while keshi pearls are created by accident.

Japanese Akoya keshi are becoming more and more difficult to find because of recent decreases in Japanese Akoya pearl production, but some other types of keshi are becoming more available due to the increase in overall production of freshwater pearls and black, white and yellow South Sea pearls. Akoya keshi are sent for processing to countries with low labor costs because the majority of Akoya keshi are very small or thin and thus have smaller-than-usual holes that must be drilled by hand without using any power tools.

In summary the term "keshi" has been used to refer to five different types of pearls. They are:

1. **Natural seed pearls**. The term "keshi" was used for these pearls before cultured pearls ever existed.
2. **Pearls that form as by-products of the Japanese Akoya pearl oyster culturing process** from nacre secretion around microorganisms or shell particles that enter the pearl during pearl nucleation. The nacre may also be secreted around detached fragments of mantle tissue inserted with the pearl nuclei. The Akoya oyster has only one grafting and one harvest of cultured pearls and keshi.
3. **Pearls that form as by-products of the South Sea and black pearl oyster culturing process.** These oysters can have up to two re-seedings of nuclei, and thus produce up to three pearls during the oyster's life cycle. Keshi pearls can be found in all three harvests.
4. **Tiny seed-like pearls that form as by-products of the freshwater pearl culturing process** from microorganisms or particles of shell or mud. These are found in the first or second harvest of freshwater pearl mussels.
5. **Chinese reborn freshwater pearls**, which are found in the second harvest. These are keshi-type pearls but not true keshi because they're intentionally cultivated—not formed accidentally. Nevertheless, they're sometimes sold as keshi by dealers.

Fig. 3.17 Natural scallop pearls (lion's paw pearls). *Pearls and photo from Pacific Coast Pearls.*

Fig. 3.18 Shell portrait cameo carved and photographed by Mikhail Smolkin

Because of the confusing use of the term "keshi" and the fact that their origin cannot be proved, labs such as the GIA Gem Trade Lab don't identify keshi on their lab reports. They simply call them cultured pearls.

Scallop "Pearls" Natural "pearls" from the scallop *"Nodipecten subnodosus."* Some people call them "lion's paw pearls" because they come from a scallop whose shell resembles a lion's paw. Until the year 2000, no one in the gem industry had ever seen a natural pearl from this scallop.

Scallop "pearls," which are found off the coast of California, range in colors from white to deep royal purple with varying shades of oranges, pinks and plums. They are non-nacreous with a mosaic pattern that has a flash effect similar to the flame-lake pattern on a conch and melo pearl. These latter two "pearls," however, are found in univalve snails instead of in a bivalve scallop. Scallop pearls range in price from $50 to $1000 per carat wholesale.

Mother of Pearl The smooth, hard pearly lining on the interior of a mollusk shell, which is used to make decorative objects, buttons and beads. Cultured pearls are a lot more expensive than mother-of-pearl beads even though pearl nacre and mother of pearl are composed of basically the same pearly substance ($CaCO_3$ and a little water and conchiolin, a binding agent). Mother of pearl, however, generally has a slightly higher percentage of water and conchiolin than pearl nacre.

There are many new designs on the market featuring mother of pearl. Mother of pearl and oyster shells are also used for carving (see figure 3.18).

Mikimoto pearls A brand name for pearls produced and marketed by the Mikimoto Co. Even though Mikimoto pearls come in a range of qualities, they are known for having a higher luster and fewer flaws than the average Akoya pearl. Mikimoto (America) Co., Ltd. estimates that only the top 3–5% of all cultured pearls harvested in Japan meet the strict requirements for carrying their trademark clasp. There are other companies, too, which sell pearls of the same high quality standards as those of Mikimoto.

Consumers should be aware that the Mikimoto name has been misrepresented in some jewelry stores and some discount places. Therefore, you shouldn't assume that pearls with a label saying "Mikimoto" are Mikimoto pearls. Look at the clasp. Only those pearls with an 18-karat-gold Mikimoto signature clasp are true Mikimoto pearls. Either a pearl or a diamond will be in the center of it. Also, when you buy Mikimoto pearls, ask the jeweler for the Mikimoto certificate of authenticity that should come with them.

Fig. 3.19 A Mikimoto clasp. *Photo courtesy Mikimoto (America), Ltd.*

The founder of Mikimoto Pearls, Kokichi Mikimoto, was a pearl farmer, researcher and merchant who brought respectability to the cultured pearl. In essence, he is the founder of the cultured pearl industry. He is also credited with inventing most of the techniques of oyster farming used today. Using some of Mikimoto's methods, Tatsuhei Mise and Tokichi Nishikawa in 1907, each became the first to invent techniques for culturing round pearls.

In the early 1900's when round cultured pearls were first sold to the public, they were considered by some as fraudulent imitations. In 1921, suits were filed in London and Paris to prevent Mikimoto from selling his cultured pearls. Mikimoto responded by filing suit to stop people from selling imitation pearls as cultured, and he persuaded the French Customs Bureau to charge the same import duty on both natural and cultured pearls. Cultured pearls had previously been classed as costume jewelry. Mikimoto also spent a great deal of time worldwide educating the jewelry trade and the general public about cultured pearls. As a result, cultured pearls became a desirable commodity and are no longer considered imitations. And Mikimoto, son of a poor noodle vendor, came to be known as "The Pearl King."

Pearls Produced by Snails

Abalone pearls Even though the abalone is not an oyster or mussel, the colorful nacreous gems it occasionally produces are considered to be pearls. This is because they consist of many concentric layers of nacre. Technically the abalone is classified as a large snail of the genus *Haliotis*.

Abalone pearls are found in abalone off the coast of California, Oregon, Alaska, Mexico, Japan, Korea, South Africa, Australia, and New Zealand. (New Zealand abalone mabe pearls are sometimes just called Paua mabe pearls because they are from the Paua abalone). Abalone pearls usually have unique baroque shapes which are sought after by designers, and their colors may be any combination or shade of green, blue, pink, purple, silver, or on rare occasions cream white. Blue and pink colors are especially appreciated. Fine-quality abalone pearls have an almost metallic-like luster and may vary in price from

Above: **Fig. 3.20** Natural pearl bracelet featuring a 156.45 carat abalone pearl. Designed and handmade by Jean Jung. *Photo from Pacific Coast Pearls.*

Right: **Fig. 3.21** Gem-quality abalone pearls ranging in weight from 40–130 cts and in price from $500–$2000 ct retail. The natural pearl jewelry was designed and handmade by Caughie. *Photo from Pacific Coast Pearls.*

Below: **Fig. 3.22** Abalone mabe pearls from Blue River Gems and Jewelry. The shell backing is showing on the underside of the drop-shape mabe.

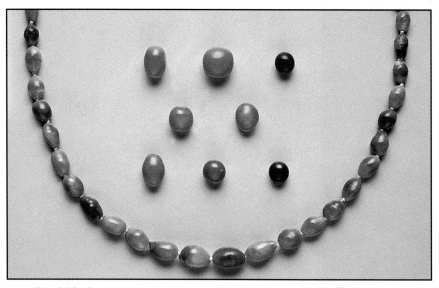

Fig. 3.23 Conch "pearls," which are found in conch shells like the one on the right.   **Fig. 3.24** Conch shell
Photos and "pearls" courtesy Mikimoto (America) Ltd.

$200 to $2000 and higher per carat depending on size and quality. Their size can range from seed size to 685 carats, the world's largest abalone pearl. It's in the personal collection of K.C. Bell and is listed in the Guiness Book of Records.

No matter what their size, abalone pearls are rare. Wes Rankin, a dealer who specializes in abalone pearls, estimates that the odds of finding a natural pearl of any size or shape in an abalone is one in 50,000.

Abalone blister pearls are being successfully cultivated, but there have been problems culturing whole abalone pearls. Abalone blood does not coagulate, so when a whole pearl nucleus is surgically implanted into the body of the abalone, it tends to bleed to death.

No surgical cutting is required to produce cultured blister pearls. A nucleus (usually a half-spherical plastic bead) is simply cemented to the inside of the abalone shell, which the abalone later covers with nacre. After a blister pearl is harvested, the nucleus is removed, the hollow area is filled with an artificial substance, and a hard backing is placed over it. It is then sold as a cultured abalone mabe pearl.

Conch "pearls" Also called "pink pearls"—though many are brownish or white— they are found in the great Conch (Strombus gigas), a large marine snail found throughout the Caribbean. Gemologists consider these "pearls" to be technically a calcareous concretion because their formation is not concentric layers of nacre. They have a porcelain-like surface.

The most valued conch pearls are symmetrical and have a distinct flame-like pattern and a strong pink or peach color. Because of the rarity of the conch pearl, even small, pale, irregular ones can retail for over $500 per carat. Better quality conch pearls may sell for over $2000 per carat and tend to be most appreciated by Europeans and Arabs.

Non-nacreous conch pearls are exceedingly rare, the average being one for every fifty thousand conches. World conch stocks are depleted because of over-

27

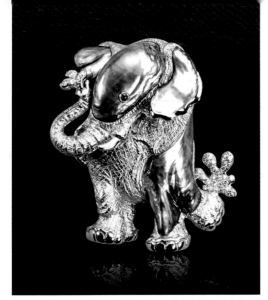

Fig. 3.25 Natural abalone pearls from Pacific Coast Pearls. *Pin, Janatello Designs; photo, Steve Walters.*

Fig. 3.26 Conch pearl and green sapphire ring by Eve Alfillé, designed so conch pearl swivels to show both sides of pearl. *Photo, Matt Arden.*

Fig. 3.27 New Zealand Paua mabe pearls. *Earrings, Eve Alfillé; photo: Matt Arden.*

Fig. 3.28 World's largest abalone pearl—685 carats. *Photo & pearl from KC Bell.*

Fig. 3.29 A polished Korean opal-like blister pearl, a product of abalone perliculture induced by electric acupuncture. *Photo by Matthew Arden.*

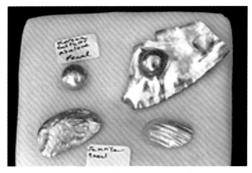

Fig. 3.30 Top: Korean cultured whole and mabe abalone pearls. Bottom: a strange pearl formation and a striated mabe produced in a Korean abalone. *Photo, Matthew Arden.*

Fig. 3.31 Faceted dyed freshwater pearls from Divina Pearls. *Photo by Cristina Gregory.*

Fig. 3.32 Faceted Tahitian cultured pearl. *Ring by Mark Schneider Design; photo by Daniel Van Rossen*

fishing, and several countries now control fishing quotas or ban the taking of conch outright.

Melo Pearls

Form inside sea snails called bailer shells, melon shells or boat shells (*melo melo*), which are found in the South China Sea and off Singapore and Malaysia. Like conch "pearls," they're non-nacreous, extremely rare and available only as natural pearls. Melo "pearls" are usually oval or round and come in orange, yellow or brownish colors with a wavy pattern. They're typically very large, weighing up to over 200 carats.

Faceted Pearls

Pearls used to be just smooth and unpolished, but recently more and more faceted pearls have appeared on the market. The faceting creates a sparkling effect and allows pearl producers to polish away flaws that would otherwise detract from the beauty of the pearl (figs 3.31, 32).

Faceted freshwater pearls are available in a wide variety of treated and untreated colors.

Gem-studded pearls

Another creative way of eliminating pearl flaws is to drill them away and set the drilled areas with diamonds or colored gems. Gem-studded pearls have a distinctive look that's made them popular with jewelry designers.

Fig. 3.33 South Sea pearls from King Plutarco Inc studded with colored gems. *Photograph by Richard Rubins.*

Judging Shape

Shape plays a major role in determining the price of pearls. Throughout history, round has generally been considered the most valuable shape for a pearl. Perhaps this was because pearls were considered a symbol of the moon. Nevertheless, the most famous and valuable pearls are often not round. That's because factors such as size, luster and origin are also important.

Akoya pearls can be divided into four basic shape categories (fig. 3.34):

♦ **Round**   So symmetrical that the pearl will roll in a straight line on a flat inclined surface. Normally the most expensive shape.

♦ **Off-Round**   Slightly flattened or ovalish

♦ **Semi-Baroque**   Obviously not round. Pear, drop, egg and button shapes are examples.

♦ **Baroque**   Very distorted and irregular in shape. Often the surface is very uneven. They occasionally resemble familiar objects such as teeth, mushrooms, cacti, tadpoles, or snails.

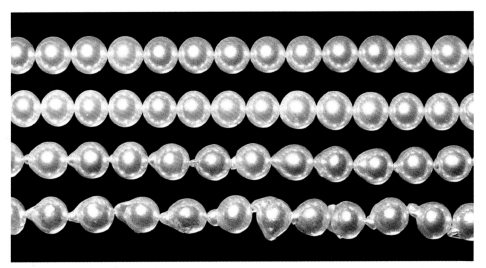

Fig. 3.34 Top to bottom—round, slightly off round, semi-baroque and baroque shapes

Sometimes additional categories are added for evaluating shape. For example, the sub-categories of "mostly round" and "slightly off-round" may also be used along with the four basic categories above.

Akoya pearl prices are generally based on round pearls. When the pearls deviate from the round shape, they are discounted. Baroque pearls, for example, may be sold for 55% to 80% less than rounds. Pearl pricing varies from one dealer to another.

When judging pearls for shape, take into consideration the type of pearl you are looking at. For example, expensive natural pearls are typically baroque, whereas cheap cultured pearls with thin nacre (pearl coating) are generally round. That's because natural pearls don't contain a round nucleus bead, and cultured pearl beads that are hardly coated with nacre don't have much of a chance to grow irregular. The typical shapes of five pearl types are described below to help you learn what degree of roundness to expect of pearls. They are listed from the most commonly round to the most commonly baroque.

Akoya pearls with thin nacre	Often round
Akoya pearls with thick nacre	Frequently off-round, but round ones are available too. Baroque Akoya pearl strands are considered low quality.
South Sea cultured	Rarely perfectly round. The larger the pearl, the more it will tend to deviate from round. Baroques are often regarded as a good alternative to the more expensive symmetrical shapes when one's budget is limited. More detailed information and photos on South-Sea pearl shapes can be found in Chapter 9.
Natural saltwater	Usually baroque or semi-baroque. Round ones are extremely rare.
Freshwater, cultured & natural	Frequently baroque, especially if they are natural. Baroque freshwater pearls are considered desirable. Cultured off-round freshwater pearls are also readily available. They are normally much more affordable than saltwater pearls of similar quality and size.

Another grading factor to consider when judging off-round and especially semi-baroque pearls is their **degree of symmetry** (perfectly round pearls are always symmetrical and baroque pearls are by definition unsymmetrical). If for example, you are buying a teardrop pearl pendant for someone special, one with two equal sides would probably be the most desirable. Lopsided pearls can be interesting, but they are considered less valuable than those which are symmetrical.

Even though dealers agree round is the most expensive shape, there is no standardized system for determining how shape affects pearl prices. As previously mentioned, the way pearls are discounted for shape variation can differ from one dealer to another. Don't let this lack of standardization lead you to ignore pearl shape as a value factor. Consider it important, and keep in mind when judging pearl prices that it's best to compare pearls of the same shape as well as the same size, color, type and luster.

4

Judging Luster & Nacre Thickness

"PEARLS—HALF OFF!"

Does this indicate a bargain? Who knows? It might even mean "Nacre—Half Off." No matter what their price, pearls aren't much of a bargain if they're dull-looking or their nacre (pearl coating, pronounced NAY-ker) peels away.

Normally thin nacre means low luster, but there are thin-nacre pearls with good luster and thick-nacre pearls with low luster. Consequently, it's best to treat luster and nacre thickness as two separate value factors.

What is Pearl Luster?

The noted gemologist, Robert Webster, defines **luster** as the surface brilliancy of a gemstone, which depends on the quality and quantity of the reflected light. When the term "luster" is applied to pearls, it tends to have a broader meaning. It also refers to the light reflected off the internal layers of nacre. In other words, a lustrous pearl has more than just a shiny, reflective surface. It also has a glow from within.

Compare, for example, the pearl to a highly polished gold bead. The gold bead will usually have sharper surface reflections than the pearl, but that doesn't mean it's more lustrous. In fact, it's more conventional to describe gold as shiny, bright or metallic. Brilliant pearls, on the other hand, are more frequently termed lustrous.

Pearls with a very high luster will generally show the following characteristics when viewed under a bare light with the naked eye.

♦ Strong light reflections
♦ Sharp light reflections
♦ A good contrast between the bright and darker areas of the pearl

(Many pearl experts would also list iridescence as a characteristic because lustrous pearls not only reflect light, they break it up into different colors. On round pearls the iridescence tends to be very subtle, and a pinkish tone may result. On high luster baroque pearls, you may see flashes of rainbow colors. Since iridescence is a color phenomenon, this book has it listed as a quality factor in the chapter on color.)

The evaluation of luster will be discussed in a later section. But first, it's helpful to know why pearls vary in luster.

What Determines Luster?

The luster of a pearl depends on the quality of the nacre—its transparency, smoothness and overall thickness as well as the thickness of each of the microscopic layers of nacre. Under an electron microscope, the nacre crystals of lustrous pearls have a strong hexagonal form and are

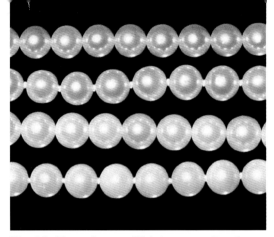 

Fig. 4.1 Top to bottom: High luster, medium luster, low luster and very low luster. Note how the dark areas become lighter as the luster decreases.

Fig. 4.2 Same pearls viewed against a white background.

regularly distributed, whereas the crystals forming the nacre of lifeless pearls lack a clear outline, are thinly scattered or are irregularly deposited (from *The Retail Jeweller's Guide*, p 90, by Kenneth Blakemore).

The quality of the nacre, and in turn the luster, is affected by a variety of factors such as:
◆ Cultivation techniques used
◆ Cultivation place
◆ Health of mother oyster
◆ Length of time pearl is in oyster
◆ Time of year when pearl is harvested
◆ Pollution
◆ Abnormally wide variations in temperature
◆ Natural disasters such as earthquakes and typhoons
◆ Type of oyster used. For example, the mabe oyster (found mainly in the tropical seas of Southeast Asia) can produce a pearl with a higher luster than those of the South Seas silver-lip oyster. The Akoya oyster is also noted for its capacity to produce pearls of high luster.

High luster is not merely the result of leaving a pearl in an Akoya oyster for an adequate length of time. As one can infer from the above list, cultivating a lustrous pearl is a complex process, and it involves skill and chance.

Judging Luster

Suppose we could line up all the pearls in the world according to the quality of their luster. We would notice that a very low percentage of the pearls would be at the end of the line with the best luster. We would also notice that the pearls would very gradually change in luster as we went down the line. In other words, there would be no distinct luster categories.

We could, however, divide the line of pearls into any number of equal ranges (categories) of luster. Then we could assign a luster name to each category such as **very high**, **high**, **medium**, **low and very low**. Luster categories like this are used by many gemologists and appraisers. Pearl dealers have their own in-house grading systems, which often combine various value factors. However, many dealers might feel that the terms **"gem quality"** or **"AAAA"** should only be applied to pearls having an exceptionally high luster. Don't assume, though, that a pearl strand labeled "AAAA" or

"Gem" is necessarily top quality. It's a common practice to misuse grades by applying high ones to lower quality goods.

Very high luster pearls have sharp, intense, almost mirror-like light reflections, and there is a high contrast between their bright and dark areas. Such pearls are not always easy to find. In fact, you may be lucky to find a store in your area that has them in stock. Expect to pay premium prices for these pearls. For example, strands of very-high-luster, round, white Akoya pearls over 6 1/2 mm won't be priced in the hundreds of dollars; they'll be in the thousands of dollars. The actual cost of the strands will be determined by a variety of factors.

Very low luster pearls are easy to spot. They look very milky or chalky, and seem more like a white bead than a pearl. This is due to the low contrast between the light and dark areas of the pearls. Some jewelers won't stock this type of pearl, but others will. This is also the type of pearl a mail order place might be tempted to sell. The customer doesn't see what he's getting. He only sees the super low price listed in the catalogue.

The majority of the pearls sold in stores probably fall in the low and medium luster ranges. Many fine-quality jewelry stores also stock high-luster pearls. The best way to learn to recognize high-, medium-, and low-luster pearls is to look at strands representing these luster ranges. Some jewelers may show you short master strands illustrating these or similar categories, but they may use different category names such as "bright," "commercial," "AAA," etc. Top-quality pearl salespeople are eager to help you see luster differences so you'll know what you are getting for your money. They don't want their prices unfairly compared to stores offering low-quality "bargain" pearls.

The latest GIA Pearl description system now lists just four categories of luster:

♦ Excellent—Reflections are bright, sharp, and distinct
♦ Good—Reflections are bright but not sharp, and they are slightly hazy around the edges
♦ Fair—Reflections are weak, hazy, and blurred
♦ Poor—Reflections are dim and diffused

As you shop for pearls and examine them for luster, keep in mind that the pearl industry has not yet adopted a standardized system for grading pearls. What one jeweler considers low or fair luster another might call medium or good luster. Therefore, **don't rely just on word descriptions of pearls.** What your eyes see is what counts most. Verbal descriptions are merely guides. If you have any strands of pearls at home, it's a good idea to take them along and use them as a basis for comparison. Even pearl dealers rely on comparison strands when buying pearls.

Also keep in mind the following tips when shopping:

♦ Examine the strands on a flat white surface, e.g. a white cloth, board or paper. Luster can be hard to judge when pearls are on a dark surface or suspended.

♦ Look at the light reflections on the pearls. Usually, the less sharp and intense they are, the lower the luster. Sometimes, however, a lack of sharpness is due to surface blemishes, rather than the overall luster.

♦ If possible, examine the pearls directly under a light instead of away from the light. This helps bring out their luster. (Lighting is discussed more in detail in the next section).

♦ Look for the brightest and darkest areas of the pearls. Then compare the contrast between the two. The lower the contrast and the milkier the pearl, the lower the luster. This is one of the quickest and easiest ways to spot low and very low luster. Milky-looking pearls are sometimes sold in "high quality" stores. Be aware that their luster is low.

♦ Compare the lusters of the individual pearls on the strand. They will almost always vary somewhat in luster. The luster quality of a strand is determined by its overall appearance, not just by one pearl. High-luster strands, however, should not have low- and very-low-luster pearls. If you find a strand you like that happens to have a pearl or two with an obviously lower luster than the rest of the strand, ask the salesperson to have them changed when they are strung with a clasp.

♦ Roll the pearls slightly so you can see their entire surface. The luster not only varies from pearl to pearl. It varies on each pearl.

♦ Try the pearls on and check if you can see the highlighted spots on them from a distance (say 10 feet/3 meters). You'll be able to if the pearls are of good quality.

♦ If possible, lay the pearls alongside other strands and compare the lusters. This is most effective when you already know the relative quality of the comparison strands. Keep in mind that your impression of a strand will be affected by the pearls it is compared to. A strand will look better when viewed next to lower-luster strands than next to those of higher luster.

Sometimes buyers get so involved in examining the shape and blemishes of pearls that they overlook their luster. The Japan Pearl Exporters' Association would consider this a big mistake. According to their booklet *Cultured Pearls*, "The most important value point in pearls of equal size is luster because that is what gives a pearl its beauty."

How Lighting Affects Luster

Gemologists and appraisers normally grade pearls under standardized lighting conditions. When shopping for pearls, you will encounter various lighting situations. You need to understand, therefore, how lighting affects the appearance of pearls in order to avoid being misled.

The main thing to remember is the stronger and more direct the light, the more lustrous the pearls will look. Ask yourself:

♦ Is the lighting diffused? For example, is the light covered with a white shade? Is the light coming through curtains, clouds or translucent glass? Is it a fluorescent light instead of a bare bulb? The more diffused the light is, the lower the luster will appear to be. Bare lights or direct sunlight, on the other hand, will bring out the luster of pearls (figs. 4.2 to 4.4).

♦ How intense is the light? In the case of sunlight, is it early morning or midday? Midday sunlight will bring out the luster more. In the case of light bulbs, are they 60 watt or 150 watt? The higher the wattage, the more lustrous your pearls will look.

♦ How close is the light to the pearls? The further the light is from the pearls, the smaller and less intense the reflections become and the less the pearls seem to glow (figs. 4.2 & 4.3). If it's possible for you to carry or wear comparison strands of pearls, do so. You'll be able to compare known strands with unknown ones under equal lighting conditions, and it will be easier for you to tell the effect of the lighting on both.

How Lighting Affects Pearl Color and Luster

Fig. 4.3 Mabe pearls ranging from high to low luster viewed under a 100-watt light bulb 4 feet (1.2 meters) away. The double light reflections are caused by an uncovered mirror in the background.

Fig. 4.4 Same pearls under a lamp with a 100- watt light bulb 1 foot (30 cm) away. The light reflection is stronger, the luster appears higher, and the overtones are more noticeable.

Fig. 4.5 Same pearls under a lamp with a 100 watt bulb diffused with paper and viewed 1 foot (30 cm) away. The diffusion reduces luster and the strength of the overtone colors.

Judging Nacre Thickness

If you were to cut a 7-mm Akoya cultured pearl in half, you would see a large core inside. It would be a bead probably cut from an American mussel shell. The outside of the bead would be encircled with a pearly layer of nacre. If the pearl had been left in the oyster for just six months, the layer would be very thin, too thin to be very durable or lustrous.

Before about 1960, Japanese Akoya pearl farmers left the pearls in the oyster for at least two and a half years. Mikimoto left his in for over three years for maximum nacre thickness. Then many farmers dropped the time to one and a half years. Around 1979, pearl harvesting started to be done just after six to eight months. The result—a lot of inexpensive, low-quality pearls on the market. And they are still out there, being offered at rock-bottom prices. The buyers end up with shell beads and hardly any pearl. Fortunately, better pearls with thicker nacre are also available, but rarely as thick as those cultured before the 1960's. The goal of this section is to help you determine if the nacre thickness of the pearls you look at is acceptable or not.

The GIA (Gemological Institute of America) defined 5 levels of nacre thickness for Akoya cultured pearls in their pearl grading course which was copyrighted in 1990:

Very thick At least 0.5 mm on all the pearls of the strand

Thick At least 0.5 mm on most pearls of the strand

Medium 0.35–0.5 mm on most pearls

Thin 0.25–0.35 mm on most pearls

Very thin 0.25 mm or less on most pearls

The GIA's latest categorization of nacre quality (2001) has just three classifications:

Acceptable—Nucleus not noticeable, no chalky appearance

Nucleus visible—The cultured pearl shows evidence of its bead nucleus through the nacre

Chalky appearance—The cultured pearl has a dull appearance

Pearl dealers don't need to measure the nacre to determine if it's thin or very thin. They know just by looking at the pearls. Some clues are:

♦ The pearls usually have a low or very low luster and may look milky. Some thin-coated pearls, however, may show a decent medium luster.

♦ The nacre coating has cracks.

♦ Areas are visible where the nacre has peeled off (figs. 4.6 & 4.7)

♦ Layers of the shell beads are slightly visible when the pearls are suspended and light shines through them. These layers look like curved lines, stripes or wood grain. Usually the thinner the nacre, the easier it is to see the lines. Figure 4.8 is an example of what the shell layers look like in a thinly-coated pearl with light shining through it. If you can't see any shell layers, this does not mean that the nacre is thick. There are lots of thinly-coated pearls that don't show these layers. However, if you can see them, the nacre is probably too thin.

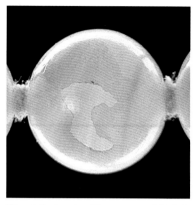

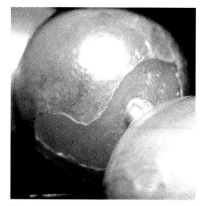

Fig. 4.6 Pearl with nacre so thin it is peeling off

Fig. 4.7 Pearl with very thin nacre peeling off around the drill hole

♦ As the beads are rolled, some may look light and then dark as the light shines through them. This is because the shell beads may have mother-of-pearl layers that block the light. This phenomenon is called "blinking" and can sometimes be seen in thinly coated pearls. Figure 4.8 is an example of two pearls with very thin nacre in the light position and dark position. When rotated, each of these pearls "blinks." Pearls with thick nacre should not blink.

A more accurate way of judging nacre thickness is by examining the drill holes of the pearls (figs 4.7 & 4.9), preferably with a 10-power magnifier such as a jeweler's hand loupe. (If you are seriously interested in gems, you should own a fully-corrected, 10-power, triplet loupe. You can buy them at jewelry supply stores. Plan on paying at least $25 for a good loupe).

Examining drill holes with a loupe will also help you detect dyes and imitations. The drill-hole method is too slow to be practical for dealers, but it is a good way for less-skilled people to estimate nacre thickness. It also allows appraisers to give a more objective measure of nacre thickness.

If you have some pearls at home, try examining their drill holes with a loupe under a good light. Find the dividing line between the nacre and the bead. Then look at a millimeter ruler with the loupe to get a visual image of a 0.35-mm thickness. Compare this thickness to that of the nacre. Seeing actual examples of thin, medium and thick nacres is an easier way to learn to tell the difference.

This book suggests 0.35 mm as a minimum nacre thickness because it has been mentioned in the trade as a minimum. For example, Hiroshi Komatsu of the Tokyo Mikimoto research lab is quoted as saying, "Our tests show the best luster and color occur with at least 0.35 mm of nacre, and Mikimoto pearls are always thicker" (as quoted by Fred Ward in the August 1985 issue of *National Geographic*). Keep in mind that the nacre thickness may not be the same throughout a pearl. Nacre measurements can also vary depending on the measuring instrument used and the person doing the measuring. So consider the 0.35-mm minimum as an approximate thickness.

When you have your pearls appraised, ask if nacre thickness is indicated on the report. Also ask how the appraiser's nacre-thickness categories are defined in terms of millimeter thickness. A term such as "thin" can vary from one person to another, so definitions are necessary. There must be a drill hole or other opening on a pearl for an accurate estimate of nacre thickness to be made visually.

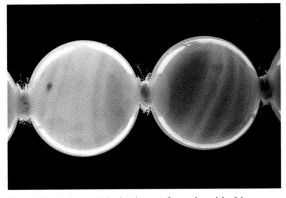
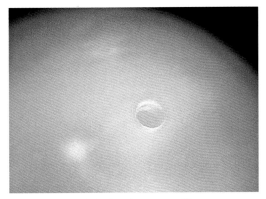

Fig. 4.8 Light and dark views of pearls with thin nacre. Note the curved stripes which indicate the growth layers of the shell bead nucleus.

Fig. 4.9 Drill-hole showing acceptable nacre thickness

Also make sure that the millimeter thickness is of the radius of the pearl, not of the diameter, which would be twice the nacre thickness along the radius. If someone tells you the average nacre thickness of an Akoya pearl is 1 mm, figure they have doubled it. Today it's hard to find Akoya pearls with even a 0.4-mm thickness.

It's not deceptive to sell thin-nacre pearls as long as the thin nacre and its consequences are disclosed to buyers. Ideally, consumers could choose from a wide range of nacre thicknesses and know exactly what they were getting for their money. Since this ideal does not currently exist, it's to your advantage to pay attention to nacre thickness and to learn to detect thin nacre yourself.

Is Nacre Thickness Important and Does it Affect Pricing?

As you shop, you may encounter pearl salespeople who claim nacre thickness is unimportant and has no effect upon price. Beware. All their pearls may be of low quality. Ask them, "Why is something which affects the beauty and durability of my pearls unimportant?"

As for price, it has to be affected by nacre thickness. It naturally will cost a farmer progressively more to culture pearls for 6 months, 1 year and 1 1/2 years. The additional cost must be passed on to the buyers.

Often the effect of nacre thickness on price is linked to that of luster. Thicker nacre usually means higher luster, and both bring higher prices.

The Mikimoto Company thinks nacre thickness is important. One of their advisors, Shigeru Miki, made the following statement in the August 1985 *National Geographic* article by Fred Ward: "The most important quality of a cultured pearl is thickness of the nacre. It gives color, luster, and appearance. Pearls are among the softest of all gems, and normal body fluids, as well as contact with perfumes, hair sprays, and acids reduce nacre. A thinly coated pearl won't last many years."

Golay Buchel, a company with branches in Europe, North America and the Orient, discusses luster and nacre thickness in its booklet *Pearls*. They are listed as separate value factors and both are described as important. Golay Buchel's advice to consumers (p. 34): "Remain flexible with regards to colour, size, shape and light surface markings, but **never** make concessions regarding the thickness of the coating."

Fig. 5.1 White & cream-colored Akoya pearls. *Photo & pearls from Hikari South Sea Pearl Co.*

5

Judging Color

If you were buying Swiss cheese and you had a choice between some that was white and some that was slightly yellow or cream color, which would you choose? Most likely the cream color because the average person has been conditioned to expect Swiss cheese to have a yellowish tint. If when you bought Swiss cheese, you discovered that pieces with large holes often tasted better than those without, you might also develop a preference for Swiss cheese with big holes.

People's expectation of what pearls should look like have been conditioned in a similar manner. Many expect pearls to be white because that's what they are accustomed to seeing. In addition, pearls are associated with the moon, weddings and purity—which, in turn, are connected to the color white.

Within the jewelry trade, Akoya or Persian Gulf pearls with high luster were often found to have a pinkish tint. Consequently, many people developed a preference for pearls with a slight pink tint. To meet the demand for such pearls, producers have sometimes bleached their pearls and dyed them pink.

There are many factors to consider when choosing the color of pearls. The topic of color will also be addressed in the chapters on freshwater, black and South Sea pearls. The Akoya pearl is the main focus of this chapter.

Pearl Color

Pearl color is complex. It's a combination of the following:

Body Color The predominant basic color of the pearl.

Overtone The one or more colors that overlie the body color. On black pearls these colors are usually easiest to see in the lighter areas of the pearl. On white pearls they are easier to see in the darker areas.

    For example, lay some white pearls on something white, and look at them under a strong, direct light (midday sun is ideal but a light bulb will do). The outer rim area of the pearls, which is reflecting the white background, will be lighter than the center of the pearls if they are of decent quality (except for the bright reflection of the light). If you look closely, you should see a slight pink, green, blue and/or silver color in the central dark areas of the pearls. This is the overtone. Generally you will see more than one overtone color in a strand

Fig. 5.2 Pearls with various body and overtone colors viewed under a bare light-bulb

Fig. 5.3 Tahitian pearls with various body and overtone colors viewed under a bare light-bulb

of pearls (fig. 5.5). You may also see more than one on the same pearl. For example, the South Sea pearl in figure 5.6 and the Tahitian pearl in figure 5.7 have both pink and green overtones. In figure 5.9, some pearls have both pink and blue overtones.

Iridescence A play of lustrous colors. They may be like those of the rainbow, or they may be a subtle combination of colors such as pink, blue, green and silver as seen in the blister mabe pearls of figures 5.8 and 5.9. The colors of the pearls change when you move them in your hand.

Orient is another term that is used to refer to pearl iridescence. In a handout from their pearl grading course, the GIA

Fig. 5.9 Some iridescent mabe pearls from King's Ransom. *Photo by Ron Fortier.*

specifies that "orient has 6 colors: violet, blue, red, green, yellow, orange, all the colors of the rainbow." Some dealers, however, employ the term more loosely to also mean a combination of overtone colors.

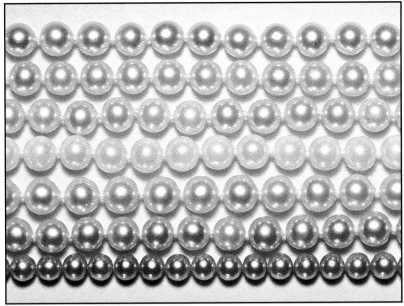

light pink—pink overtones

white—pink & green overtones

white—green & silver overtones

low quality white

cream—mostly pink overtones

yellow—various overtones

dyed yellow (golden)

Fig. 5.5 Akoya pearls come in a range of colors. Specifying pearl color, however, is not easy. Body color, overtones and iridescence must all be considered. To complicate matters, the pearls within a strand vary in color.

Fig. 5.6 Green & pink overtones on a South Sea pearl

Fig. 5.7 An example of pink and green overtones on a Tahitian black pearl button clasp. These overtones are frequently found together on high-quality black pearls. The absence of overtones is a sign of low quality. *Photo courtesy of Assael International.*

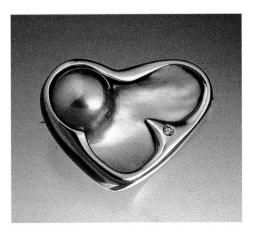

Fig.. 5.8 Tahitian mabe blister brooch with iridescent colors

Fig. 5.10 Top-quality pearls are colorful, like an oyster shell. These mabe and Akoya pearls have a light pink body color with blue and pink overtones. As you move the pearls, they appear to change color due to their pearly iridescence. The overtone colors are most apparent when the pearls are viewed against a white background under a strong direct light such as a light-bulb. Broad diffused lighting tends to whiten pearls.

Other dealers and many books written in the past use the term "orient" to refer to luster because iridescence and luster are interconnected. Since "orient" may be interpreted in various ways, this book tends to use the term "iridescence" instead.

When you shop for pearls, you may come across terms such as **white rosé**. This means white pearls with a pink overtone. "Rosé" is the French word for pink. **Pink rosé** means that most of the pearls have a light pink body color and a pink overtone. White pearls with a silver overtone may be described as **silver(y) white**. Often salespeople don't specify the overtone but they just say one color such as "pink" which describes their overall impression of the pearls.

Judging Pearl Color

When deciding what color pearls to buy, your primary concern should be what looks best on you. But you will also want to know how the color affects their price.

The overall body color can play a significant role in determining the price of Akoya pearls. Five main **body color categories** for pearls are:

Light pink (pink)   Usually the highest price category, but some dealers price light pink and white pearls alike. A few dealers make a distinction between pearls with subtle pink tints and those that look artificial and obviously dyed. They may refuse to stock the latter. Incidentally, jewelers often have no way of knowing if their pink pearls are dyed because suppliers are not required to disclose this. Naturally-colored pink pearls, however, typically have a light pink rather than a pink body color.

White Equal to or less than pearls with a light pink body color. Some people in the trade have a negative view of "white pearls" because they associate them with the very thin-nacre pearls that look milky white and have no overtone. It's not the white body color that makes these pearls appear low-quality; it's the absence of overtones, as seen in the middle strand of figure 5.5. Lustrous, valuable pearls normally have silver or pink overtones.

Light Cream Usually cost less than white. The higher the quality of the pearls, the greater the price difference will probably be between light cream and white. In low qualities, there may be no difference.

Cream Usually cost less than light cream. In cream colors, the general tendency is the darker the color, the lower the price. Cream-color pearls are sometimes termed **champagne pearls**.

Dark Cream & Yellow May be priced about 40% or more lower than white Akoya pearls. The darker darker the cream or yellow color, the greater the price difference.

When judging color, keep in mind that there is no standardized system of communicating or grading color in the pearl industry. What one dealer calls light cream, another might call cream. Nevertheless, there is an awareness of the concept "cream color" and general agreement that cream-color Akoya pearls tend to cost less than those which are pink or white.

Overtone color(s) may or may not affect the price. The three most common overtones are pink, green and silver. If the color of the overtones has an effect on price, it will generally be as follows:

Pink overtones Can increase the price

Silver overtones Usually no effect

Green overtones Sometimes may decrease the price slightly

The combination of blue and pink overtones is associated with top-quality pearls. Some Japanese dealers describe the color of the most valued Akoya pearls as a bluish-pink, which in essence is a light-pink body color with blue and pink overtones. These pearls, which are extremely rare and difficult to find in America, are sometimes classified by the Japanese as "hanadama quality."

There is no general agreement in the trade as to how overtones affect price. Most dealers, however, would probably concede that Akoya pearls with pink overtones tend to be more highly valued than those with green ones. This explains why pearls are often dyed pink but not green. What counts most about overtone is how it affects your overall impression of the color and luster of the pearls. Pearl dealers would agree, too, that the presence of overtones is highly desirable. Their absence is a sign of low luster and thin nacre.

The third color component of pearls, **iridescence**, is rarely obvious on round Akoya pearls. It tends to be very subtle combination of pink, blue and green. A more obvious iridescence—flashes of rainbow colors—is more likely to be seen on freshwater pearls and baroque shapes. Iridescence is always considered a positive value factor.

When examining pearls for color remember the following tips:

♦ Judge the color of pearls against a non-reflective white background. Pearls not only reflect the color of the background, they also absorb it. Afterwards, place the pearls on your hand or around your neck to see how they look on you.

♦ Take into consideration the lighting (see next section). If possible look at the pearls under different types of light sources—daylight near a window, fluorescent, and incandescent (light bulbs). You'll probably be wearing the pearls under a variety of light sources.

♦ It's a lot easier to compare color than to remember it. If possible, wear or take along some comparison pearls. Otherwise, compare the color to other pearls in the store. Even using white and cream-colored papers as color references is better than relying on color memory.

♦ When pearl strands are exactly adjacent, their color may seem to bleed from one strand to another. Therefore, also compare them slightly separated from each other.

♦ Every now and then, look away from the pearls at other colors and objects. When you focus on one color too long, your perception of it becomes distorted.

♦ Consider how evenly distributed the color is on the pearl(s), especially if it's one major pearl on a ring or pendant. A uniform color is more highly valued than a blotchy one.

♦ If you are trying to decide between white and pink pearls of the same quality but the pink pearls cost more. Look in a few of the drill holes with a 10-power magnifier. If you can see red or pink stains on the nacre layer or a pink line between the nacre and the nucleus, they are dyed (see Chapter 12 about treatments). Seeing positive indications of dye may influence your decision. By the way, even if you don't see evidence of dye, the pearls may still be dyed.

♦ Make sure you're alert and feel good when you examine pearls. If you're tired, sick or under the influence of alcohol or drugs, your perception of color will be impaired.

How Lighting Affects Color

Just as luster is affected by lighting, so is color, but in a different way. If you were to take a photograph indoors under a light bulb with daylight film, the picture would be orangy or yellowish. If you took it under fluorescent light, the picture would look greenish. Even though, unlike cameras, your eyes can adjust to changes of color from lighting, you're still influenced by them. Consequently, your perception of pearl color will depend on the lighting under which the pearls are viewed.

The whitest, most neutral light is at midday. Besides adding the least amount of color, this light makes it easier to see various nuances of color. Consequently, you should judge pearl color under a daylight-equivalent light. Neutral fluorescent bulbs approximate this ideal, but some of these lights are better than others. Three that are recommended are the Duro-Test Vita light, GE Chroma 50 or Sylvania Design 50. This light, however, is not as effective as true sunlight for seeing detail. For example, it's normally easier to read very fine print in sunlight than in artificial light. The intensity of the light from the sun has a lot to do with this.

When you shop for pearls, your choice of lighting will probably be limited. Use the information below to help you compensate for improper lighting.

Type of Lighting	Effect of Lighting on Pearl Color
Sunlight	Depends on the time of day, season of the year, and geographic location. At midday it normally has a neutral effect on the hue. Earlier and later in the day, it adds red, orange or yellow, so the pearls may look pinker or yellower.
Incandescent light bulbs, halogen spotlights and candlelight	Add red. Pearls may look pinker or more yellowish.
Fluorescent lights	Depends on what type they are. Most intensify blue colors. Warm white tubes add yellow.
Light under an overcast sky or in the shade	Adds blue and gray, so pearls may look grayish or a bit bluish.

Emphasis on proper lighting when viewing gems has not been restricted to modern-day times. In 1908, in *The Book of the Pearl* (p. 370), Kunz and Stevenson wrote:

"At great receptions, large and apparently magnificent pearls are frequently seen, which are really of inferior quality, and yet owing to the absence of pure daylight, they can easily be mistaken for perfect specimens by any one not especially familiar with pearls. Indeed, if the royalties of Europe should wear all the pearls belonging to the crown jewels at the same time, in a palace or hall lighted with candles, gas, or even with some types of electric light, they would seem to have a quality which many of them do not and never did possess. It is, therefore, essential for the buyer to use every precaution in reference to the light in which he examines his purchase."

What Causes Pearl Color?

A lot of pearl farmers wish they had the full answer to this question. Then they could control the color of the pearls they cultivated. Now they have only part answers or clues. Some of the determinants of pearl color seem to be:

♦ The type of host oyster. Oysters vary in their potential to produce certain colored pearls. For example, black pearls are cultivated in the black-lip oyster because other oysters don't produce pearls of the same type. Even though pearl farmers know the black-lip oyster is essential to the cultivation of black pearls, they don't know yet how to consistently make it produce a specific color. The pearl may end up being white or a variety of shades of gray as well as black, bronze, greenish or purplish.

♦ The quality of the nacre. If the nacre is very thin, the color will look milky and lack overtone tints. Besides being affected by the number of layers of nacre, pearl color is affected by the thickness of each layer. In *Pearls of the World* (p. 71), researcher Koji Wada states, "The reason why the pearl made by the Akoya pearl-oyster has a better pink tone than pearls made by other mollusks is that it has layers of equal thickness."

♦ The environment in which they are grown. It's theorized that there may be trace elements in the water that affect the color. For example, cream-color pearls are typical of natural pearls from the Ohio River, but not of those found in other American Rivers.

Pearls: the Wedding Jewel

The tradition of giving pearls to brides probably dates back to about 1000 BC when the Hindu God Krishna gave his daughter pearls on her wedding day. It continued with the ancient Greeks, who believed that pearls would ensure a happy marriage. The association between pearls and weddings reached a peak during the 14th and 15th centuries when everyone from the bride to her male guests were adorned in pearls.

Today pearls, which symbolize purity and innocence, are as much a wedding jewel as diamonds. Just have a look at a bridal shop or wedding catalogue. You'll find pearls, both fake and real, decorating wedding gowns, veils, tiaras, gloves, purses, ring-bearer pillows, cake toppers and party favors. And at weddings, you'll notice that pearls have become essential jewelry for both the bride and bridesmaids.

Pearls of Wisdom from a Wedding Expert

Jet Taylor of J Taylor Bridal Jewels in Charlotte, North Carolina has advised brides for years on their bridal attire. Here are some of her tips on selecting wedding pearls:

● The bride's pearl jewelry should be well matched. For example, her pearl earrings should be of the same type and color as her pearl necklace. The bride is the featured attraction, so she should expect that her guests will be closely examining everything she's wearing on this special day.

● Pearl jewelry should be color-coordinated with the pearls on the gown rather than with the gown itself. For example, if the gown is ivory-colored and the pearls on it are white, the bride's pearl jewelry should also be white. The pearls on the gown should be the same color as those on the veil. In sum, all the pearls the bride is wearing should look like they were made to go together.

● If the bride would like to wear a necklace, earrings or brooch from her grandmother that doesn't match her other pearls, consider placing a note in the program stating the bride is wearing, for example, a pearl necklace in honor of her grandmother.

● If a bride or bridesmaid is wearing a necklace, it should be at least one inch above the neckline so it will not look as if it is going to fall into the dress. If the necklace is longer, it should be at least two inches below the neckline so that it will show and the necklace cannot fall into the dress

● Despite the above tips, the bride should remember that this is her day and she has a right to wear whatever she wishes.

tissue inserted in Akoya oysters is yellow, cream-colored pearls tend to form. If white, white pearls result (*Modern Jeweler*, September 1990, pp. 42-44, David Federman).

What Color is Best for You?

Most pearl experts agree that a buyer's color choice should be primarily based on what will look good on the person who will wear the pearls. Some salespeople, though, give color advice by suggesting what's popular in specific geographic areas. One fairly consistent statement, for example, is that South Americans prefer cream- or golden-colored pearls.

When shopping in the United States, the color listed as the number one choice may vary from one salesperson to another. Perhaps it's a matter of what the store has in stock. It's sometimes claimed that the most popular pearl color in America is pink. The U.S., however, is a diverse nation. Consequently, pink is not the color that looks best on all Americans. Picking a color on the basis of its popularity might lead to a poor choice.

Determining the colors that flatter you most is not always easy. Carole Jackson, in her book, *Color Me Beautiful*, provides some guidelines with color illustrations. She points out on page 28, for example, that olive-skinned people and most blacks and Orientals look radiant in clear, vivid, cool colors (pink, white, blue, red) but sallow in warm colors (cream, orange, beige, mustard). Warm colors, however, are very flattering to people with peach or golden complexions (Redheads and blondes often have this skin coloring).

Some people in the trade recommend white and pink pearls to Asians and Anglos and cream or golden pearls to blacks and olive-skinned customers. This is because cream colors look whiter on a dark-skinned person than on someone with lighter skin.

One easy way to determine which pearl colors will compliment you is to put on white, light pink, and cream-colored clothing and see what looks best next to your face. It's helpful to get the opinion of family and friends. Often, two of the colors look equally attractive, but it's rare that all three will. The final test will be to put the pearls on your hand or around your neck and see how they look. Consider, too, if you want people to notice the pearls when you wear them. If you do, then choose a color that contrasts with your skin tone. Pearls that blend in too closely won't be very striking.

When you're buying for others, they probably won't be able to try on the pearls. So beforehand, observe what color clothes they like to wear and look good in. If they don't like beige or cream-colored clothes and these colors don't flatter them, you' be better off avoiding cream-colored pearls.

Two other considerations when choosing pearl color are versatility and price. If you would like to wear the pearls as often as possible, then select colors that will go well with most of your wardrobe. If your budget is limited and you are trying to choose between light or dark cream pearls, the dark cream pearls could be the ideal choice. Don't buy them, though, if cream colors make you look washed out. The purpose of jewelry is to enhance your appearance, not detract from it. So put some thought into your color choices. It will pay off in the end.

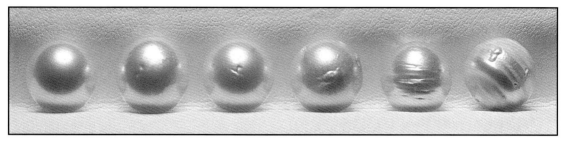

Fig. 6.1 Pearls ranging from clean to very heavily blemished

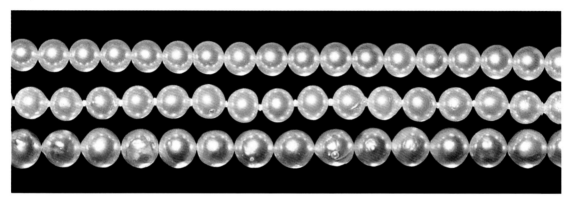

Fig. 6.2 Surface comparison photo. Top strand—relatively clean (unblemished), middle strand—moderately blemished, bottom strand—heavily blemished.

Fig. 6.3 Enlarged view of same strands

6

Judging Surface Quality

Imagine that you're buying a bouquet of roses for a special friend. If you were to look closely at each rose, you would probably notice some brown spots, small holes or torn edges. Yet it's doubtful that any of these flaws would keep you from getting the bouquet. You would select it on the basis of its overall attractiveness.

However, if you were buying just one rose for somebody, you would most likely examine it more closely and expect it to have fewer flaws than the roses in a bouquet. Judging pearls is much the same. Our standards of perfection for a single pearl are normally higher than for a strand. But whether we're dealing with roses or pearls, we should expect nature to leave some sort of autograph.

When discussing flaws in diamonds or colored gems, the jewelry trade uses the term **clarity**. This refers to the degree to which a stone is flawed. In the pearl industry, a variety of terms is used. For example:

Blemish	Spotting
Cleanliness or Cleanness	Surface quality
Complexion	Surface appearance
Flawlessness	Surface perfection
Purity	Texture

In the USA, **surface quality** is the term most frequently used to denote pearl clarity.

There are also a variety of synonyms for the term "flaw:"

Blemish
Imperfection
Irregularity
Spot
Surface characteristic
Surface mark or marking

When dealing with diamonds and colored gems, gemologists limit the term "blemish" to surface flaws such as scratches and bumps. The term "inclusion" refers to flaws that extend below the surface such as cracks and holes.

"**Blemish**" takes on a different meaning when used with pearls. It means any kind of flaw, internal or external. This book often uses the term "flaw" because it's short and easily understood by the trade and general public. For the sake of variety, other terms are used as well.

Flaws can be positive features. They serve as identifying marks that a gem is ours and not somebody else's. They help prove that it is real and not imitation. Flaws can lower the price of gems without affecting their overall beauty. Perfection does not seem to be a goal of nature. In fact, the longer a pearl is in an oyster, the more likely it is for irregularities to occur. Therefore, when shopping for pearls, there's no need to look for flawless ones. You just need to know what types of imperfections to avoid.

Pearl Blemishes

A standardized terminology has not been developed for pearl blemishes. The terms found below are based primarily on those listed in the GIA (Gemological Institute of America) pearl grading course. These imperfections are usually judged without magnification.

Fig. 6.4 Some typical pearl blemishes—pits, bumps, welts, holes, pinpoints and a dull white area

♦ **Bumps and Welts:** Raised areas which are found alone or in groups. They may sometimes cover most of the surface area of the pearl. If bumps or welts are very large, they can put the pearl into the off-round category. Occasionally pearls have a wrinkled appearance. This is due to groupings of welts.

♦ **Discolorations:** Spotty areas often caused from concentrations of conchiolin, a protein substance that holds nacre crystals together. Discolorations are not frequently seen because pearls are typically bleached to even out their color.

♦ **Chips, Holes and Patches of Missing Nacre:** Blemishes which may occur on any type of pearl but that are particularly common on those with thin nacre.

♦ **Pits and Pinpoints:** Tiny holes on the surface which are normally hardly noticeable and, therefore, not serious. "Pinpoints" may also refer to tiny bumps since, from a distance, these look about the same as tiny pits.

♦ **Dimples:** Circular depressions or indentations which are often found in groups.

♦ **Dull Spots:** Areas of very low luster due to variations in nacre quality or contact with chemicals, cosmetics or skin secretions.

♦ **Cracks:** Breaks in the nacre and/or bead nucleus. Small cracks in the bead may look like little hairs trapped under the nacre. Cracks, even when not visible, can threaten the durability of a pearl.

♦ **Scratches:** Straight or crooked lines scraped on the pearl. These aren't serious unless the pearl is so badly scratched the luster and beauty is affected.

Determining Which Blemishes Are Acceptable and Which Aren't

It's not the presence of flaws that matters. It's the type, quantity and prominence of the flaws that does. Listed below are blemishes which would normally be considered unacceptable:

◆ **Cracks throughout the pearls.** Thick nacre does not crack easily. Thin nacre does. Even if the cracks aren't noticeable, they are a sign that the nacre is too thin and that the pearls won't give you lasting wear.

◆ **Patches of missing nacre.** Just as diamonds with big chips are considered unacceptable, so are pearls with chunks of missing nacre. Both the beauty and durability of the pearl are affected.

Fig. 6.5 Missing nacre around the drill hole

◆ **Prominent flaws on a single pearl.** When buying pearl earrings, pendants, pins or rings pay closer attention to the flaws. For example, a pearl with a large, visible bump would not be acceptable as the featured pearl of a jewelry piece, but it would be okay in a strand. If you are buying an expensive pearl and you want to compromise on price, try to select one whose imperfections can be hidden by the setting.

◆ **Obvious discolorations throughout the pearls.** For the sake of beauty, try to select pearls with a uniform color. There are plenty of them available.

◆ **Blemishes which cover the majority of the surface of the pearl.** They can cause a viewer's attention to be directed more at the blemishes than at the pearls. Figures 6.6 and 6.7 are examples of how groups of minor flaws over a large surface area become more noticeable and therefore less acceptable.

Fig. 6.6 A group of minor pits

Fig. 6.7 A group of tiny welts

53

Despite the undesirability of blemishes, if you had to choose between heavily flawed, lustrous pearls and near flawless pearls with very thin nacre and low luster, you would be better off with the flawed ones. At least you would be getting some pearl for your money.

Keep in mind when buying pearls that it's not just their inherent quality that determines their acceptability. Your needs and desires also count. If you're looking for a fine quality necklace, you'll want to avoid strands with noticeable flaws. If your budget is limited, you'll probably be glad that there are blemished pearls available at reduced prices. You have the final say as to what's acceptable and what's not.

Tips On Judging Surface Quality

When you shop for diamonds, salespeople may suggest that you look at the stone under magnification so you'll know its clarity. This won't happen when you shop for pearls. The reason jewelers don't have you view them under a microscope is because pearls are graded and valued on the basis of how they look to the naked eye, not under magnification (except nacre thickness).

When dealing with knowledgeable salespeople who have your interests at heart, you won't have to look at pearls with a loupe (hand magnifier). They will point out the imperfections and other quality factors and show you how to compare pearls. But there are times when it is advisable to use a loupe:

♦ **When dealing with people you don't know or who may not be trustworthy**. Suppose you are at a flea market or an antique show and you see a pearl piece you'd love to have that you would never find in a jewelry store. Or, suppose you are on vacation abroad and you want a souvenir but you don't know any jewelers and none have been recommended to you. In both cases, it would be advisable to use a loupe and check for flaws, thin nacre, dye and imitations. The more experienced you become at examining a pearl's surface and drill holes with a loupe, the easier it will be for you to identify pearls and judge their quality.

♦ **When the lighting is poor**. Suppose you're an antique dealer or a pawnbroker and you're in a place where the lighting is not ideal. And suppose you have to make a quick decision about whether to buy some pearls and how much to offer. Poor lighting will make it harder to judge surface quality and detect imitations. Use a loupe as a means of compensating for the lack of proper lighting.

♦ **Whenever pearls are being offered at a price that seems too good to be true.** There's usually a catch somewhere. It will probably be easier to find it with a loupe than with the unaided eye, especially for people who don't deal with pearls on a regular basis.

A few other pointers for judging imperfections are listed below:

♦ Besides looking at the pearls against a white background, look at them against a dark one. Certain flaws show up better against black or other dark colors. Also hold the pearls in the air to examine them for flaws. Do not judge luster or color in this way, however.

♦ Examine the pearls under a strong light. The more intense the light, the easier it is to see detail. When judging blemish, it's also a good idea to look at pearls under different types of lighting—bare/diffused, fluorescent/incandescent, close/distant. Each type may bring out different details in the pearls.

♦ Roll the pearls. Otherwise you may not see some serious flaws and you won't know what percentage of the pearls is flawed. An anecdote by Kunz & Stevenson in *The Book of the Pearl* (p. 371) illustrates the importance of looking at all sides of the pearls.

> "A pearl necklace valued at $200,000, shown at one of our recent great expositions, was, to all appearances, a remarkably beautiful collection, and it was only when the intending purchaser took them from their velvet bed and held them in his hands that he realized that there was not a perfect pearl in the entire collection. It must have taken more than a week of study for the clever dealer to arrange them so that the best part, sometimes the only good part of each pearl, should be where the eye would fall upon it. After they had been turned in the hands a few seconds, not one perfect specimen was visible."

♦ Keep in mind that it's normal for pearls to have a few flaws.

Grading Surface Quality

The diamond industry has a standardized system for grading clarity based on a system developed by the GIA. Ten-power magnification is used. The advantage of having this system is that buyers can communicate what they want anywhere in the world. In addition, written appraisals and quality reports are more meaningful. The GIA has tried to establish such a system for pearls. Their latest system defines four categories of surface quality:

♦ Clean—Pearls are blemish-free or contain minute surface characteristics that are very difficult to see by a trained observer. .

♦ Lightly blemished—Pearls show minor surface irregularities when examined by a trained observer.

♦ Moderately blemished—Pearls show noticeable surface characteristics

♦ Heavily blemished—Pearls show obvious surface irregularities that might affect durability.

Most pearl dealers have their own systems for grading surface quality. Occasionally you'll come across grades such as AAA, AA, A. Depending on the supplier or store, these grades may refer to the luster, the flaws, a combination of these two factors, or they may include other factors such as shape and nacre thickness. In essence, pearl grades have no meaning except what the seller assigns to them. Therefore, do not rely on grades to compare pearl prices. Examine the pearls yourself, use your own judgment and consider the following:

♦ **The prominence of the blemishes**. Visible flaws away from drill holes are more serious than those near the holes. High bumps can be more noticeable than small pits or low bumps.

♦ **The type of flaws.** Chipped or missing nacre is usually more serious than bumps even though it may be less noticeable.

♦ **The percentage of the pearl surface that is flawed**. It's a lot more serious if 80% of the surface of a pearl is flawed than if only 10% of it is. You need to roll the pearls to check this factor.

♦ **The percentage of pearls on a strand that are flawed and to what degree**. This is a factor that doesn't exist in diamond grading. Pearl grading is more complex. It's much harder to develop consistent grades for sets of gems than for single gems.

7

Size, Weight, Length

Size

The size of round saltwater cultured pearls is expressed in terms of their diameter measured in millimeters. One millimeter is about 1/25 of an inch. Since pearl size varies within a strand, a range of ½ millimeter is usually indicated, e.g. 7– 7 ½ mm. Occasionally, a few of the pearls might fall slightly above or below the size indicated. Usually the larger the size, the higher the price.

The size of non-round pearls can be expressed in terms of their greatest width and length and in some cases depth. The measurements are generally rounded to the nearest half or whole millimeter.

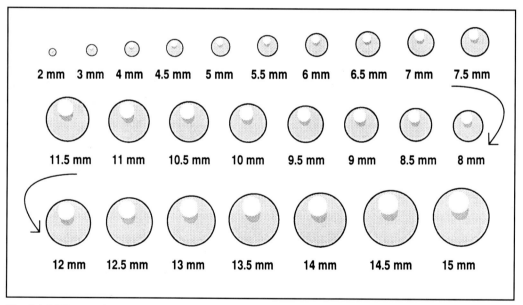

Fig. 7.1 Millimeter sizes. *Diagram by Dawn King.*

When determining the effect of size on price, keep in mind the following.

◆ Price jumps between pearl sizes are often uneven. As the sizes reach the 8 or 9 mm mark, pearl prices tend to jump more.

◆ Price/size relationships can vary from one dealer to another.

56

♦ The effect of size on price varies from one harvest to another. If too many pearls of one size are harvested, their price will go down.

♦ Demand can have an important impact on the way size affects price. If there's a high demand for a specific size, its price tends to increase. This explains why occasionally smaller pearls sell for more than bigger ones of the same quality.

Weight

When pearl wholesalers buy large lots of cultured pearls, they are often charged according to the weight of the pearls. The measure generally used is the **momme**, an ancient Japanese unit of weight which equals 3.75 grams or 18.75 carats. **Kan** is a Japanese unit of weight equaling 1000 momme. Pearls are not sold by the momme or kan in retail stores.

The size of natural pearls is often expressed in pearl grains. One **grain** equals 0.25 carat. Natural American freshwater pearls may be sold according to their carat weight. The **gram** is commonly used to express the weight of cultured freshwater pearls, although carat weight is also used. One **carat** = 1/5 gram. Or in other words 5 carats = 1 gram. Weight equivalences are summarized in Table 7.1. The approximate weight of individual loose pearls can be calculated by referring to both Tables 7.1 and 7.2.

Table 7.1 Weight Conversions

1 carat (ct)	= 0.2 g = 0.007 oz av = 4 p grains = 0.053 m
1 gram (g)	= 5 cts = 0.035 oz av = 20 p grains = 0.266 m
1 ounce avoirdupois (oz av)	= 28.3495 g = 141.75 cts = 565 p grains = 7.56 m
1 pearl grain (p grain)	= 0.05 g = 0.25 ct = 0.013 m = 0.0017 oz av
1 momme (m)	= 3.75 g = 18.75 cts = 75 p grains = 0.131 oz av

Table 7.2 (Based on data from the Shima Pearl Co.)

Size	Pieces Per Momme	Size	Pieces Per Momme
2.5 mm	160 pcs	6.5 mm	9.3 pcs
3 mm	90 pcs	7 mm	7 pcs
3.5 mm	63 pcs	7.5 mm	6 pcs
4 mm	40 pcs	8 mm	5 pcs
4.5 mm	27 pcs	8.5 mm	4.2 pcs
5 mm	19 pcs	9 mm	3.5 pcs
5.5 mm	15 pcs	9.5 mm	3 pcs
6 mm	12 pcs	10 mm	2.5 pcs

Length

When pricing pearls, you should take into consideration the length of the strand as well as the millimeter size of the pearls. The pearl trade has specific names for different necklace lengths. They are as follows:

1. Choker
A 14–16 inch (35–40 cm) necklace whose central pearl normally lies in the hollow of the throat or just below it. It looks especially attractive with V-neck blouses and dresses.

2. Princess
A 16–20 inch (40–50 cm) necklace. This slightly longer length is well suited for pearl enhancers (detachable pendants) and can slenderize the neck.

3. Matinee
A 20–26 inch (50–66 cm) necklace. Some people like to wear a matinee length along with a choker. Or they have it strung with two hidden (mystery) clasps so it can also be worn as a bracelet and a shorter necklace.

4. Opera
A necklace about twice the size of a choker.

5. Rope
A necklace longer than an opera length. The defined length will vary according to the jeweler or company using the term.

Courtesy Mikimoto Co.

Pearl necklace lengths are summarized in the following list:

1.	Choker	14–16"	35–40 cm
2.	Princess	16–20"	40–50 cm
3.	Matinee	20–26"	50–66 cm
4.	Opera	28–36"	70–90 cm
5.	Rope	40" +	1 meter and longer

The preceding lengths are approximate. Definitions of necklace-length terms can vary from one jeweler to another. Keep in mind that pearl strands become slightly longer (about 2 inches or 5 cm) when knotted and strung with a clasp to form a necklace. The following table will help you determine approximately how many pearls there are in a 14" and 16" strand.

Table 7.3 (Based on data from the Shima Pearl Co.)

Size	Pearls per 14" strand	Pearls per 16" strand
2.5–3 mm	130	148
3–3.5 mm	110	125
3.5–4 mm	97	110
4–4.5 mm	83	95
4.5–5 mm	76	87
5–5.5 mm	70	80
5.5–6 mm	63	72
6–6.5 mm	57	65
6.5–7 mm	53	60
7–7.5 mm	50	57
7.5–8 mm	46	52
8–8.5 mm	43	49
8.5–9 mm	41	47
9–9.5 mm	39	44
9.5–10 mm	36	41

Strands with pearls over 10 mm (South Sea pearls) are usually longer than 16."

There are some other terms relating to pearl necklaces that consumers might not be familiar with. They are:

Bib A necklace of three or more concentric strands. The lowest strand normally does not fall below a matinee length.

Dog collar A multi-strand choker-length necklace. The strands may be clasped together in a single clasp. "Dog collars" help conceal neck wrinkles.

Torsade A multi-strand necklace formed by twisting strands around each other. This is a popular way to wear freshwater pearl strands.

Uniform strand A strand whose pearls are all about the same size.

Graduated strand A strand with pearls of different sizes which gradually get larger towards the center. Graduated strands provide a big pearl look at a lower price than uniform strands.

Fig. 7.2 Dog-collar. *Photo from the Cultured Pearl Associations of America and Japan.*

Judging Make

Imagine spending fifteen years collecting over 30,000 pearls just to find the right pearls for one necklace. Someone in Texas took the trouble to do this. A picture of the resulting necklace can be seen in color figure 8.1. The pearls on the strand have a variable fair to very good luster, most are round but some are off-round, they range in size from 3.70 mm to 8.15 mm, and their color ranges from brownish to purplish pink with a few pearls being pinkish orange.

This necklace could be classified as having an unusually fine make. Why? Because all of the pearls on the necklace were natural freshwater pearls recovered from lakes and rivers in West Texas. And it's amazing that so many pearls of this type could be so round and blend together so well. When judging make we have to take into account availability of the pearls being graded.

Fig. 8.1 Strand of natural freshwater pearls from the San Angelo area of West Texas (3.79 to 8.15 mm). These pearls were collected over a period of 15 years. *Photo courtesy Gemological Institute of America. Photo by Shane McClure.*

Make is a combination of the following factors:

♦ How well the pearls match or blend together in terms of color, shape, luster, size and surface perfection

♦ How centered the drill holes are

♦ How smooth the size increase is of pearls in graduated strands

Some dealers charge a premium that may range from 1%–15% for Akoya strands that are of very fine make. Others may discount them if the pearls don't match very well. Premiums of up to 30% or more can be charged for well-matched pairs of large, high quality natural or South Sea pearls. It can take a great deal of time and luck to find pearls that match.

Fine make is relative, though, and buyers should be flexible about their expectations. One should not expect South Sea, freshwater or natural pearls to be as round and match as well as cultured Akoya pearls.

The definitions of what constitutes good, fair and poor make in Akoya pearl strands can vary from one dealer to another. Some may emphasize color most. Uniform luster, size and/or shape may be more important to other dealers, even though they would probably all agree that the overall appearance is what counts. An example of what dealers would agree is a poorly matched Akoya strand can be found in figure 8.2. Figure 8.3 is an example of a well-matched strand and pendant.

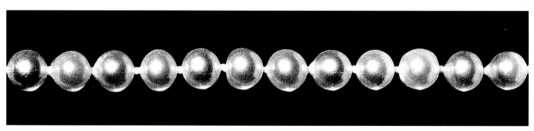

Fig. 8.2 Poorly matched strand

As mentioned earlier, it's important to take into account the availability of the pearls being graded when judging make. This means that:

♦ Non-dyed pinkish strands should not be graded as strictly for make as a non-dyed cream-colored strand since cream colors are more plentiful.

♦ Dyed and non-dyed Akoya strands should not be graded alike since it's a lot easier to match dyed pearls than those that aren't.

♦ Very-thick-nacre pearls shouldn't be discounted as much for shape variations as thin- and medium-nacre pearls since pearls that are in the oyster longer have a greater chance of growing irregular.

We must be careful not to become so concerned about perfect matching that we end up down-playing other quality factors. We should also make sure that we are realistic about our expectations.

Fig. 8.3 Well matched 8–8.5 mm Akoya strand and South Sea pearl enhancer. Finding Japanese pearls that match one from the South Seas is a challenge. *Photo and necklace from Albert Asher South Sea Pearl Co.*

The author recalls being in Tokyo just after taking a pearl grading seminar. Somehow she had formed the idea that if the overtones of pearls in strands didn't match, they were unacceptable. She looked at some of the highest priced Akoya strands in some of most exclusive stores in Tokyo and was quite surprised to find not a single strand whose overtones matched. They all seemed to have a combination of green, pink and silver overtones, but the strands varied in the percentage of each color. Finally, she realized that she was being unrealistic and that as long as the body color looked uniform and the overtones blended together well and their differences weren't obvious, there was nothing wrong with the pearls.

Judging make requires a balanced perspective. On the one hand, we shouldn't be so lax that we let shoddy workmanship become the norm. On the other, we shouldn't be so perfectionistic that no pearls can meet our standards. When you look at a strand of pearls, consider its overall impact. Your attention should not be drawn away by obviously mismatched pearls. Neither is it desirable for the pearls to be lackluster but perfectly matched. Look at as many different qualities and strands of pearls as often as possible. You will form a sense of what's acceptable and eventually you'll have an appreciation for what is truly fine make.

Fig. 9.1 South Sea keshi (the two bottom strands) and Australian South Sea cultured pearls. The largest loose pearl at the top is 18 mm. South Sea cultured pearls are produced by oysters which have been implanted with a nucleus. South Sea keshi are formed accidently in oysters cultivated by man and contain no nuclei. (The term "cultured" is often omitted for the sake of brevity.) *Photo and pearls from Hikari South Sea Pearl Co.*

9

South Sea Pearls (White & Yellow)

Mallory is puzzled. At the mall, she saw a large white pearl ring in a jewelry store window for $5000. Then, in a another store window, she saw what appeared to be a ring of the same size and quality for $500. She went in and asked the salesman if it was a real pearl ring. He told her it was and suggested she try it on. She liked it, and considering the price of the other ring, felt she was getting a bargain, so she bought it. Now she is wondering why there was such a large difference in price between the two rings. Can you think of a possible explanation?

There is one. The pearl in the first ring was a whole **South Sea pearl**—a large whole pearl cultivated in a South Sea oyster. The pearl Mallory bought was a 3/4 mabe pearl—an assembled pearl, which was also probably from a South Sea oyster. A mabe pearl grows attached to the inner surface of the oyster shell. After it is cut from the shell, the nucleus bead which was inserted to make it grow is removed, and the remaining hole is filled with a paste or wax (and sometimes also a bead or colored plastic dome). Then it is covered with a mother-of-pearl backing (some bargain-priced mabes are backed with plastic). The resulting mabe pearl has a pearly nacre coating almost the same as a whole cultured pearl. The main difference is that it tends to be thinner. Consequently, some mabe pearls may crack very easily.

Even though the salesman was not wrong about the pearl being a real cultured one, he should have told Mallory it was an assembled pearl, especially since there is a vast price difference between mabe pearls and whole pearls. (Large fine-quality mabes are available for a few hundred dollars, whereas large fine-quality whole pearls can cost several thousand dollars each.)

Unfortunately, salespeople don't always disclose important information, and some sellers may not know the difference between a mabe pearl and a South Sea pearl (It should be noted that some people in the trade do not regard mabes as true pearls). No matter what their background

Fig. 9.2 South Sea mabe pearl

is, salespeople should never call mabes South Sea pearls. Only a South Sea *whole* pearl merits the price and name of "South Sea Pearl."

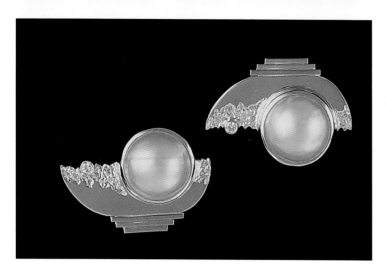

Fig 9.3 Mabe pearl earrings hand fabricated by Gary Dulac. *Photo by Azad.*

Fig. 9.4 Mabe pearl necklace which was purchased for Geena Davis. It was created by Erica Courtney. *Photo by Ralph Gabriner.*

Fig. 9.5 Mabe and freshwater pearl earrings created by Krespi & White. *Photo by Marty Kelly.*

Mabe pearls are commonly shaped like half pearls, which makes them ideal for pendants and pins. They are also grown in 3/4 shapes to make them appear more like whole pearls when set in mountings such as rings. If a mabe pearl is loose, it's easy to tell it's assembled because the mother-of-pearl backing has a different appearance than the pearl nacre (fig. 9.1). In addition, you can see the line where the backing and pearl dome were glued together. When mounted, however, a mabe pearl may look like a South Sea whole pearl or 3/4 pearl, particularly if the bottom of the pearl is encased in gold.

Assembled pearls may occasionally look like whole pearls. The winter 1989 issue of *Gems and Gemology* shows an assembled pearl which seemed to be a whole natural pearl when x-rayed (p. 240). But when it was unmounted, it became obvious that two pearl pieces had been glued together. The final GIA Gem Trade Laboratory report concluded "Assembled pearl consisting of two sections of natural pearl or blister pearls cemented together."

South Sea pearls are cultivated in a variety of places—Australia, Indonesia, the Philippines, Thailand and Burma (now called Myanmar). Currently, Indonesia is the most important producer of pearls in the 9 to 12 mm range. The main source of pearls over 12 mm has been Australia. Australia's first pearl farm was established in 1956 on the Northwest coast at Kuri Bay. Prior to that time, Australia was producing up to 75% of the world's supply of mother of pearl, and pearls were just sold as a byproduct.

The silver-lip (*Pinctada maxima*) oyster is the main oyster used in Australia to cultivate South Sea pearls. If it's healthy, it can produce up to four pearls inserted at different times. The cultivation period may range from 1 1/2 to 2 years. The oysters that are unsuitable for whole pearls or that reject the bead nucleus are used to culture mabe pearls. Most of the large white mabe assembled pearls sold are cultivated in South Sea silver-lip oysters.

Gold-colored pearls have recently become very popular, but they are rare. The yellow-lip (also called gold-lip) oyster in which they are occasionally found, normally produces light yellow and cream-colored pearls. Indonesia is the main source of yellow pearls, but they are also produced in the Philippines and Thailand.

Price Factors

South Sea pearls are priced according to their luster, color, shape, surface perfection, size and nacre thickness. But low price does not necessarily mean low quality when it comes to shape, color and size. The low price results from a greater supply and a lower demand of certain colors, shapes and sizes. Luster, nacre thickness and surface perfection, on the other hand, do affect the actual quality of pearls. More information on each of these price factors is provided below.

LUSTER:
The higher the luster, the more valuable the pearl. White South Sea pearls have a lower luster potential than Akoya pearls and Tahitian black pearls. Take this into consideration when evaluating white pearls. Figure 9.6 shows three fine quality strands with different lusters. For tips on how to judge luster, see Chapter 4. Luster and nacre thickness are the most important price factors.

COLOR:
As is the case with Akoya pearls, choice of color should be based on what will look best on the person who will wear the pearls. The color varies depending on which variety of *Pinctada maxima* oyster the pearl comes from—the silver-lip or gold-lip. The silver-lip oyster, the main oyster in

Fig. 9.6 Compare the lusters of these three fine-quality pearl strands. The almost mirror-like luster of the black strand does not occur naturally on light-colored South Sea pearls. The luster of the golden pearls falls between that of the black and white strands. *Photo and pearls from Albert Asher South Sea Pearl Co.*

Australia, tends to produce silvery white pearls. The gold-lip variety, which is more commonly found around countries such as Indonesia, Thailand and the Philippines, is more likely to produce yellow or cream-colored pearls.

The body color of South Sea pearls is judged in about the same way as it is in Akoya pearls. Usually white and pink pearls are more valued than yellowish and cream-colored pearls, but there is now one major exception. Pearls with a natural strong pinkish-yellow color that dealers identify as **golden** (can sell for as much as pinkish white pearls of the same size and quality. The more saturated the gold color, the more valuable the pearl. Light yellow colors are not highly valued. Figure 9.8 shows four South Sea

Fig. 9.7 Golden pearls from Indonesia. *Photo and earrings from Albert Asher South Sea Pearl Co..*

pearls from the gold-lip oyster that have different yellowish or gold colors. The actual colors of these pearls is probably different. Photographs do not show fine nuances of color accurately.

Fig. 9.8 Natural-color yellow pearls from Indonesia. Their price decreases as the color becomes less saturated. Strong yellow colors that look golden sell for premium prices provided the color is natural. Light yellow and cream colors cost the least.

The presence of overtones and iridescence is very desirable in South Sea pearls. In white pearls, pink and silver overtones are more highly valued than bluish-gray and greenish overtones. Bluish overtones, however, are appreciated if they are combined with pink overtones.

When buying gold South Sea pearls, be sure to ask if the color is natural. A high percentage of them are dyed and/or irradiated, especially those with strong gold or grayish-gold colors. If the color is natural, have this written on the sales receipt. It's advisable, too, to have expensive pearls checked by a gem laboratory. Read Chapter 12—Pearl Treatments.

Fig. 9.9 Some South Sea pearl shapes, right to left: round, oval, drop, button, circle, baroque. These general categories don't always give a clear visual image of shape. A better description of the circled pearl shape might be circled bullet or circled drop.

SHAPE:
The more round the pearl the more valuable it is. But round South Sea pearls are very rare, far more rare than Akoya pearls, which are smaller and have thinner nacre. The thicker nacre and longer growth periods of South Sea pearls leads to a wide variety of shapes. These cannot be described adequately with just the four Akoya shape categories of round, off-round, semi-baroque and baroque. Some of the most common terms used to describe South Sea pearl shape are as follows:

Round: So symmetrical that the pearl will roll in a straight line on a flat inclined surface. Normally the most expensive shape.

Semi-round or **off-round:** Almost round, but the pearl will wobble or deviate to one side as you roll it.

Oval: An elongated round shape. It sells for much less than rounds.

Drop: Rounded at one end and elongated or pointed at the opposite end. The extension or tail corresponds to the incision where the nucleus was inserted. There are several variations of the drop shape. A few are shown in Chapter 10 in the section on black pearl shapes. The drop shape is sometimes described as **semi-baroque**, especially if it's unsymmetrical. The more symmetrical a drop shape is, the greater its value. Very symmetrical drops with a smooth top and pleasing shape are called "perfect drops" or "knock-out drops" by some dealers.

Pear: A drop shape with a slightly concave "waist." Some people use the terms "drop" and "pear" interchangeably.

Button: Rounded on one side and flatter on the other. The width is greater than the height. Buttons generally sell for less than drops and rounded shapes except in sizes over 16 mm where they are used for earrings. A round pearl of 17 mm sticks out too far from the ear, while a button makes an ideal earring. Since there's a high demand for buttons over 16 mm, their prices are high.

Acorn: Resembles an acorn. Has a high dome shape and flat bottom (fig. 3.5 in Chapter 3). This shape is practical for earring drops and brooches, but there is less demand for it than for the button shape.

Triangle: Has a pointed or drop-shaped top and a flat bottom. Short triangles may be used for stud-type earrings, and long triangles can be used for pendants and dangling earrings.

Circle or **circled:** Have one or more parallel, ring-like furrows around the pearl. These circular formations do not occur as frequently in white and yellow South Sea pearls as in those which are dark-colored. Circled shapes sell for much less than the previous shapes. Circles or rims can be present on drops, ovals, off-rounds, triangles and buttons.

Baroque: Irregular or freeform (fig. 9.10). This shape is often preferred by designers because of its uniqueness. Generally, the baroque and circled pearls are the lowest priced of all the shapes.

No matter what their shape, South Sea pearls are generally sold undrilled if they are not on a strand. This allows the buyer to determine how the pearls will be used or mounted. Be willing to compromise on shape. This may be necessary due to the high price and limited availability of round South Sea pearls.

SURFACE PERFECTION:

South Sea pearls are graded for imperfections in the same way as Akoya pearls, except with much more leniency. The fewer the flaws the higher the price. The percentage of the surface area which is free of imperfections is also important in determining value. A South Sea pearl can often be mounted in a way that will hide its flaws when worn. This means if you select your pearl(s) carefully, you can have a clean-looking one for a lower price. Remember that blemishes on single pearls tend to be more obvious than on those in strands. Therefore, when buying a loose South Sea pearl, figure out in advance how you will wear it so you can choose one whose flaws won't be noticeable.

Fig. 9.10 Baroque South Sea pearl necklace, 24 pearls, 25 x 17 x 15.3 mm to 17 x 13 x 12.5 mm. *Photo and pearls courtesy Albert Asher South Sea Pearl Co.*

SIZE:

South Sea pearls generally range in size from 9 to 19 mm. The size of semi-round pearls is indicated by the average diameter or by the smallest measurement of the diameter. The size of baroque pearls is most accurately represented by stating the length, width and height. However, sometimes only the two largest measurements are given.

The world's largest round South Sea pearl is 24 mm. Baroque pearls can have greater length measurements than round ones. The largest pearl in the necklace of figure 9.10 is 23 mm long. The "Nugget of Australia," a pearl belonging to the collection of Golay Buchel, has a length of 25 mm and weighs 90.6 ct. (*Pearls of the World* p. 116). It's their large size that makes South Sea pearls so expensive. As would be expected, the larger the pearl the greater its value.

The size of a cultured pearl is primarily determined by the size of its bead nucleus. The bigger the oyster, the bigger bead it can accept and the bigger pearl it can grow. Consequently, small Japanese oysters which measure 4 inches (10 cm) across, produce smaller pearls than the silver or gold-lip oysters which can measure 12 inches (30 cm) across. Black-pearl oysters, which also produce white pearls, grow up to about 8 inches (20 cm) across and produce a pearl in between the size of the silver-lip and Akoya oysters.

South Sea pearl strands aren't normally sold in the same ½ mm increments as Akoya pearls. They're usually graduated with larger pearls in the center and smaller pearls on the ends. It's very difficult to find matched South Sea pearls of one size. In addition, it's not cost effective to place large pearls at the back of the neck where they aren't necessarily seen. Consequently, it's best to give a size range when asking for South Sea pearl strands—for example, 12–14 mm. The most typical Australian South Sea strand size is probably 11–13 or 14 mm. Dealer's will do special strand layouts such as 12–13 mm or 14–15 mm on request. But these are costly, and a deposit may be required before the dealer will make up the strand.

NACRE THICKNESS:

Big pearls do not necessarily have thick nacre. As with Akoya pearls, the nacre thickness of cultured South Sea pearls has decreased during the past 30 years. In the April 1971 issue of *Lapidary Journal*, Australian pearl farmer C. Denis George stated that a good cultured South Sea pearl had a nacre thickness double the radius of the bead nucleus. In other words, a 15-mm pearl had about a 5-mm nacre thickness and a nucleus whose radius is about 2.5 mm. If this standard were used today, it would be very hard to find a good South Sea pearl. Judging from standards published by black pearl producers, South Sea pearls today should have a nacre thickness of at least 1 mm of the radius. (See nacre thickness section in Chapter 10).

One millimeter may sound thick compared to the minimum standard this book suggests for Akoya pearls—0.35 mm. Keep in mind, though, that Akoya pearls have a finer-grained nacre than South Sea pearls and they are smaller. A 0.5-mm thickness on a 6-mm Akoya pearl is 1/6 of the radius. A 1-mm thickness on a 12-mm South Sea pearl is also 1/6 of the radius. Therefore, it's reasonable for buyers to expect nacre at least 1 mm thick on their South Sea pearls, especially considering their high cost.

Thin nacre is not as easily detected in South Sea pearls as it is in Akoya pearls. Because of the thicker nacre, the shell layers of the bead do not show up as well and it's harder to see the bead nucleus through the drill hole. In addition, the pearls are often mounted in jewelry so the drill holes aren't visible. Experienced dealers can often detect thin nacre by evaluating the quality of the luster. Thin nacre pearls may have a shiny surface, but they won't have a deep lustrous glow.

To avoid buying South Sea pearls with nacre that's too thin, you should select pearls with a good luster and deal with jewelers who consider nacre thickness important. It's also a good idea to have the pearls x-rayed by a gem lab when the price of the pearls is high enough to warrant the cost of an x-ray report, which is about $100 to $300. The nacre thickness can be measured in the x-ray photograph.

Like all other pearls, those from the South Seas come in a wide range of qualities and prices. Some sell for over $20,000 and some sell for $100. The price factors above are what determine the value. For example, just take a $20,000 dollar South Sea pearl, make it smaller, add lots of flaws, give it a baroque shape, color it yellow, and give it a dull, drab luster. What can be the result? A $100 South Sea pearl.

10

Black Pearls

Black pearls are not necessarily black. More often than not they range from a light to very dark gray, but they may also look green, pink, lavender, blue or brown. It's the oyster source, not color, that determines if pearls are called black pearls. "Black pearl" is a generic term that refers to pearls from:

- Black-lipped pearl oysters (*Pinctada margaritifera*), Western to Central Pacific & Indian Oceans
- La Paz pearl oysters (*Pinctada mazatlanica*), Eastern Pacific between Baja California & Peru.
- Rainbow-lipped (western-winged) pearl oysters (*Pteria sterna*), Eastern Pacific between Baja California & Peru.

Some people mistakenly identify all black pearls as Tahitian pearls. Tahitian pearls are found in French Polynesia and they're marketed in Tahiti. Pearls from the Cook Islands are Cook Island pearls, not Tahitian pearls. Black pearls from the Gulf of California can be called La Paz pearls, Mexican pearls, Baja California pearls or simply black pearls. Some sellers call black pearls from the rainbow-lipped oyster "rainbow pearls" because of their natural rainbow-like colors.

If you go to Hong Kong, you may see strands labeled "black pearls" that sell for a couple hundred dollars. They are probably artificially colored Akoya pearls whose natural color was undesirable. In Tahiti, **"black pearls"** must be of natural color to merit the name of "black pearl" or "Tahitian pearl." The jewelers in both areas are correct in their use of the term "black pearl" as long as the treated pearls are identified as dyed, irradiated or treated black pearls. In other words, the unmodified term "black pearl" implies the pearl is of natural color.

Over 99.9% of the black pearls sold on the market today are cultured. So for the sake of brevity, this book often leaves out the term "cultured" when referring to cultured black pearls. Nowadays, when pearls are natural, they are identified as such. A few natural black pearls have been recently found in the *Pteria sterna* oyster off of Baja California (see figure 10.2). Natural pearls (those created without human intervention) are rare, so don't expect to find them in your local jewelry store.

Natural-color black pearls can be confused with natural-color "blue pearls." Unlike black pearls, whose color is an inherent characteristic of the pearl nacre, **blue pearls** derive their color from foreign contaminants in the nacre itself or between the nacre and the shell bead nucleus. Naturally-colored dark Akoya pearls are good examples of blue pearls. They may be blue, black, gray or brown. Black pearls and blue pearls can look the same but because of the difference in the origin of their color, blue pearls are worth less. The fact that blue pearls might decay or lose their color if holes are drilled through them is another reason for their lower value.

Fig. 10.1 Tahitian cultured black pearls. *Earrings, pendant and photo by Linda Quinn.*

Fig. 10.2 Natural black pearls from the rainbow-lipped oyster in the Gulf of California. *Pearls & photo from Pacific Coast Pearls.*

Since there can be a great value difference between black pearls, blue pearls and artificially colored pearls even though they may look the same, consumers need to be concerned about buying black pearls that are misrepresented. In Chapter 12, you'll see how to spot pearls that are not true black pearls. Keep in mind, though, that the only sure way to identify a natural-color black pearl is to send it to a lab and have it tested.

It's only been within the last 25 to 30 years that cultured black pearls have become commercially important. Most of them are cultivated in Tahiti (French Polynesia to be more accurate) and others are produced in places like Okinawa, Fiji, the Cook Islands and Baja California.

Natural black pearls, however, became known in Europe after Hernando Cortez and later explorers discovered colored pearls in the Gulf of California. In the late 1700's and early 1800's, La Paz in Baja California became the black pearl center of the world. Natural black pearls in the South Seas were also being fished at this time. Gradually black pearls grew quite popular, especially among European royalty, such as Empress Eugenie of France. But the oyster beds were overfished and black pearls became scarce. Then in the 1940's, a large percentage of the black pearl oysters in the Gulf of California died for unknown reasons. Within the last 15 years, there has been a gradual redevelopment of black pearl fishing and culturing in the Gulf of California between Baja California and Mainland Mexico. As a result, a few natural pearls are now being found and cultured whole and mabe black pearls are being produced there.

Fig. 10.3 Tahitian cultured pearls with a variety of of overtone colors. *Bracelet by Divina Pearls, photo by Cristina Gregory.*

Fig. 10.4 Five colorful "apples" of Tahitian cultured pearls, set around a quartz bowl carved by Dieter Lorenz. *Pin/pendant by Eve J. Alfillé; photo by Matthew Arden.*

Price Factors

Black pearls are priced according to their luster, color, shape, surface perfection, size and nacre thickness as follows:

LUSTER:

Black pearls can look almost metallic. You should expect a higher and different luster from them than you would from white South Sea pearls. Dark nacre does not reflect light in the same way that white nacre does. The best way to learn the luster potential of a black pearl is to look at some black pearls ranging from very low to very high in luster. After you compare them, you probably won't be satisfied with a black pearl of low luster, and you shouldn't be. Good luster is an essential ingredient for pearl beauty. Keep in mind that lighting can affect black pearls in the same way it does white pearls, so compare pearls under equivalent lighting conditions. (See Chapter 4 for a discussion of lighting.)

Low luster in black pearls is often correlated with thin nacre, as is the case with white pearls. But thin-nacre black pearls can have good luster and thick-nacre pearls may have low luster. Consequently, it's best to treat luster and nacre thickness as two separate value factors.

COLOR:

Twenty years ago, the preferred coloration for black pearls was dark gray with green and pink overtones (peacock colored). Tastes have changed. Lighter colored black pearls have become very popular and so have multicolored necklaces. Today, there's not much difference in price between dark "peacock-colored" pearls and the pastel-colored pearls. Brownish colors, however, are not as highly valued and neither are solid black pearls with no overtone colors.

Other overtone colors on black pearls are blue, gold, silver and a reddish purple called "aubergine," which is the French word for eggplant. Overtones may be present in a variety of combinations such as pink and green, and they are considered a plus factor. It's easiest to see the overtone colors in black pearls when the lighting is diffused and at a distance from the pearl. Bare lights close-up (e.g. ½ meter away) tend to mask the overtones in black pearls even though they bring out the overtones of white pearls.

Above: **Fig. 10.5** Tahitian black pearl button earrings (14 mm) with detachable pearl drops. Note their fine luster, symmetry, surface and green overtones. *Photo from Assael International.*

Right: **Fig. 10.6** Multicolored Tahitian pearl necklace and bracelet. It was purchased for Elizabeth Taylor. *Jewelry by Erica Courtney; photo by Ralph Gabriner.*

There is no standardized system throughout the pearl industry for classifying or valuing the color of black pearls, and considering the complexity of it, there may never be. At any rate, you should select colors that you like and that look good on you.

SHAPE:

Round and semi-round shapes are the most expensive. Drop shapes are the next most expensive followed by button shapes which are flat on one side and rounded on the other. The more symmetrical these shapes are, the more their value. Baroque shapes and circled pearls with ring-like formations around them are the least expensive. See Chapter 9 for a more detailed explanation of South Sea pearl shapes.

Fig. 10.7 Varied black pearl shapes create an interesting bracelet. *Jewelry by Erica Courtney; photo by Ralph Gabriner.*

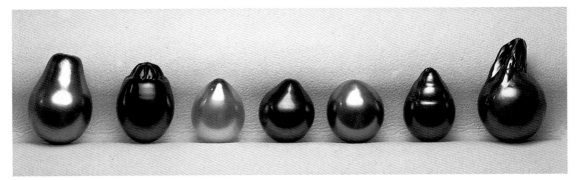

Fig. 10.8 Drops come in a wide range of shapes and sizes. The drops with the smoothest tops and most symmetrical form are usually priced the highest, all other factors being equal. Designers, however, often prefer unique, asymmetrical shapes.

When you need to cut down on the price of a black pearl, shape is a good category to compromise on. In fact, baroque and circled pearls often make more interesting jewelry pieces than round pearls do.

SIZE:
Naturally the bigger the black pearl the more expensive it is. Black pearls generally range in size from about 9 to 18 mm with their average size tending to be between 9 and 11.5 mm. Some baroque black pearls may reach 25 to 30 mm in length. Size has a great impact on price. A 1 mm increase in the size of medium-quality pearls can raise their price 100 to 200%.

Above: **Fig. 10.9** This black pearl cross shows how an odd-shaped pearl can be used creatively. *Jewelry by Erica Courtney, photo by Peter Valli.*

Left: **Fig. 10.10** Circled pearls make attractive necklaces. These strands are from King Plutarco, Inc. One has circled drop pearls and the other has pearls which are more roundish. Circled pearls are more affordable than those which are smooth.

At the retail level black pearls tend to be described and priced according to millimeter size. Weight may be used as an additional means of identifying them. This is the opposite of round diamonds where the price is based on the weight, but measurements may be given to help distinguish them from other diamonds of the same weight.

On the wholesale level, however, large lots of black pearls are sold according to their weight, which is measured in momme (1 momme = 3.75 grams = 18.75 carats). The pearls are graded into various categories, and each category is assigned a per-momme price.

SURFACE PERFECTION:

Flaws can decrease the price of black pearls considerably, which is an advantage for consumers. A black pearl can often be mounted in a way that will hide imperfections when worn.

This means if you select pearl(s) with partially flawless surfaces, you can have a clean-looking one for a lower price. Remember that blemishes on single pearls tend to be more obvious than on those in strands. It's normal for pearl strands to have some flaws.

NACRE THICKNESS:

It should be at least 1 mm (of the radius). The thicker the nacre the more valuable the pearl. As you are shopping, you may encounter salespeople who claim that all black or white pearls from the South Seas have thick nacre, and that nacre thickness need not be a consideration. Many people who specialize in producing or studying black pearls would disagree.

Dr. Jean-Paul Lintilhac, installer and developer of two black pearl farms in Tahiti, is one example. In his book, *Black Pearls of Tahiti*, he states that jewelers in Tahiti are worried about the thinness of the nacre of some of the pearls offered to them for sale. He goes on to say that certain pearl farmers are in such a hurry to recover their investment that they harvest their pearls prematurely and as a result the nacre is very thin. Then he writes (p. 85):

"Formerly a big pearl meant a good thickness of nacre, but with the supergrafts used today, size is no guarantee. If you are buying a big expensive pearl, you have the right to ask for an x-ray of it which will enable you to see and measure the thickness of the layers of nacre surrounding the nucleus. One millimeter of nacre is a minimum for a good pearl."

Tahiti Pearls, a major black pearl company, also tells consumers in their book *The Magic of the Black Pearl*, that nacre thickness is a criteria used to judge black pearls. They indicate a 1 mm to 1.5 mm nacre thickness as an appropriate range for black pearls.

Hisada and Komatsu of the Mikimoto Co. put nacre thickness at the top of their list of pearl quality factors (*Pearls of the World* p. 90). They state:

"Nacre thickness is a basic factor in judging the elegance of the pearl. Its beauty and durability depend on the thickness of the nacre, its quality and quantity."

The Mikimoto company, in their leaflet "The Art of Selecting Cultured Pearls," tells consumers: "For beautiful pearls the most important factors are luster and nacre thickness."

Chapter Four gives guidelines on determining if the nacre thickness of Akoya pearls is acceptable. Unfortunately these techniques do not work as well on black pearls. It's often impossible to see into their drill holes because the pearls may be glued to a jewelry piece such as a ring or pendant mounting. Also the nacre of black pearls may mask the layers of a shell bead nucleus that might be visible in a thin-nacre Akoya pearl. Dealers use luster as a guide to nacre thickness because a good deep luster signals good nacre thickness .

Usually the best way of determining the nacre thickness of a black pearl is with an x-ray. And, if you are spending thousands of dollars on a pearl piece, it's well worth your money to have a gem lab x-ray the piece to check for nacre thickness and to determine if the color is natural. But what should you do if you are paying, say $500 for a black pearl pendant? An x-ray in a case like this is probably not worth the money. The best thing you can do is to choose pearls with as high of a luster as possible and **buy your pearls from jewelers who consider nacre thickness important.**

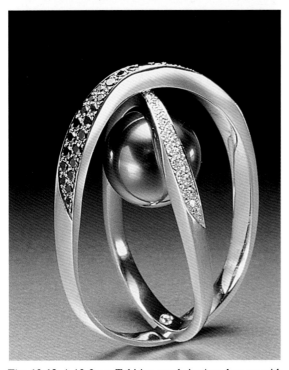

Fig. 10.12 A 12.3mm Tahitian pearl ring/pendant set with black & white diamonds. This piece by Mark Schneider Design is hinged to open & close. *Photo: MJSA.*

Fig. 10.13 A 13.5 mm Tahitian black faceted pearl ring with opal inlay, tsavorite garnets and diamonds. Ring by Mark Schneider Design. *Photo by John Parrish.*

It's often hard to understand why one pearl may cost $50, for example, and another may cost $500. But let's consider how the preceding factors might work together to lower the price. If a pearl costing $500 decreases a little in size, its price may drop 50%, to $250. Going from a very high to very low luster could make its price drop another 50% to $125. Then adding lots of flaws to the pearl could bring its price down to $50.

Pearl pricing is not as mathematically regular as this example; nevertheless, the above quality factors can have a similar effect on its price. So take them into consideration as you shop and compare prices. Also, when you look at pearl prices in ads and catalogues, remember that they are meaningless if an adequate description of the pearls isn't included.

Fig. 10.14 Tahitian pearl ring designed and photographed by Ponthieux's Jewelry Design.

Opposite page: Fig. 10.11 An array of Australian, Tahitian and Indonesian pearl strands of various colors and shapes from King Plutarco Inc. *Photo by Keith Gaynes.*

Figs. 11.1 & 11.2 Cultured Chinese freshwater pearls. *Jewelry by A & Z Pearls; photos by John Parrish.*

Fig. 11.3 Cultured Chinese freshwater pearls & Tahitian black pearls. *Jewelry by A & Z pearls; photo by John Parrish.*

11

Freshwater Pearls

The Japanese, at Lake Biwa, are credited with being the first to succeed in cultivating freshwater pearls on a commercial basis, although freshwater pearls in the shape of Buddha had been cultured in China as far back as the thirteenth century. The technical roots of cultivating freshwater pearls are attributed to Masayo Fujita, the "father of freshwater pearl cultivation" (page 136, *Pearls of the World,* article by Hidemi Takashima, a chief engineer at the Nippon Institute for Scientific Research on Pearls).

The first harvest of Biwa pearls was in August 1925 and they had a shell bead nucleus like Akoya pearls. By the 1930's they were being sold overseas. Some merchants from India would buy these Lake Biwa pearls from Fujita and then resell them to the Middle East as highly valuable Persian pearls for huge sums of money. One day, it was accidentally discovered that a shell bead is not necessary for the cultivation of a freshwater pearl. All that is needed is the insertion of a piece of mantle (a membranous tissue which secretes nacre and lines the inner shell surface of mollusks). This is a lot less trouble than inserting both a bead and mantle tissue. Also, it was noticed that after the first harvest, mussels can spontaneously grow pearls a second and third time. What this means is that cultured freshwater pearls usually have more pearl nacre than cultured Akoya pearls because most do not have a shell bead nucleus.

Pearls that are cultivated using just mantle tissue are called **tissue-nucleated pearls** in America and **non-nucleated pearls** in Britain and Commonwealth countries. When a shell bead is implanted along with a graft of mantle tissue, the resulting pearl is called a **nucleated pearl** or a **bead-nucleated pearl** (The bead can be any shape; it isn't necessarily round). The general term for any pearl cultivated in a lake, pond or river area is **freshwater cultured pearl**. For the sake of brevity, this book usually omits the word "cultured" since practically all pearls today are cultured.

Biwa pearls (pearls from Lake Biwa) have enjoyed a great deal of prestige. This is because they tend to have a smooth surface and a high, even luster. Unfortunately, production almost came to a halt in the early 1990's due to the death of most of the Biwa mussels. It is now being resumed. Some dealers still have old stocks of pearls from Lake Biwa to sell, but many pearls which are identified as Biwa pearls are actually from China.

Most freshwater pearls today are produced in China. Their quality has been steadily improving since 1991 and their sizes have been increasing. At the end of 1992, semi-round Chinese freshwater pearls made their appearance on the market and now offer an attractive, lower priced alternative to the round Akoya pearls. Some of the larger pearls are even becoming alternatives to South Sea pearls.

China and Japan are not the only places where freshwater pearls are found. There are many historical accounts about the natural freshwater pearls of Europe and North America. These pearls are still being sold, but in decreasing quantities. Overfishing, flooding and pollution has either dwindled or, in some areas, eliminated the supply of these natural pearls.

Upper left: Fig. 11.4 Rice-shaped freshwater pearls cultured in China in the 1980's. *Necklace and earrings copyright Fred & Kate Pearce, photo by Tommy Elder*

Upper right: Fig. 11.5 Chinese freshwater pearls cultured in the early 1990's. *Designs copyright by Fred & Kate Pearce, photo by Tommy Elder.*

Lower left: Fig 11.6 Natural-color 8–9mm freshwater pearls cultured in China in the early 2000's and a neckpiece of drusy quartz carved by Dieter Lorenz. *Design copyright 2003 by Fred & Kate Pearce; photo by Ralph Gabriner.*

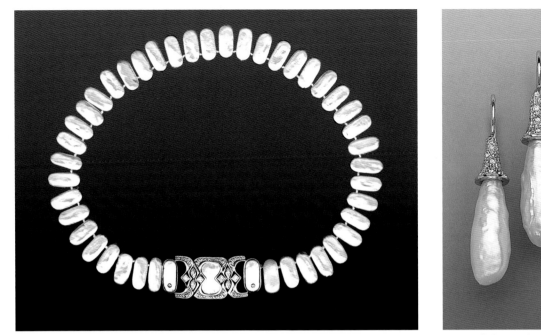

Fig. 11.7 Necklace of cultured American pearls in 18k with diamond and mother of pearl clasp. *Jewelry design copyright by Eve J. Alfillé; photo by Matthew Arden.*

Fig. 11.8 Cultured American freshwater pearls. *Earrings by Linda Quinn; photo from American Pearl Co.*

The cultured freshwater pearl market in the United States, however, is gradually increasing. They're now being cultivated in Tennessee with a shell bead nucleus. Their nacre is very thick due to the fact they are left in the mollusks for three to five years. Unlike most other freshwater pearls, American cultured pearls are never bleached, dyed or treated. You'll find them in a wide variety of shapes—marquises, drops, coins, tadpoles, domes and bars. Tennessee is also known for being the primary source of the shell bead nuclei in Akoya and South Sea pearls.

Price Factors

The grading of freshwater pearls is more variable than that of saltwater pearls. Nevertheless, there is agreement about certain value factors. Freshwater pearls are generally valued according to the following criteria:

LUSTER:
The higher and more even the luster, the greater the value. Low-quality freshwater pearls may seem lustrous to a lay person because often part of their surface is very shiny. However, if some areas of the pearls look milky, chalky and dull, they are considered to have a low luster. In high-quality freshwater pearls, there is an evenly distributed luster and a high contrast between the light and dark areas of the pearls.

When judging freshwater pearls for luster, examine them on a white background and be sure to roll them so you can see their entire surface area. If possible, compare strands of different qualities. It's important that your eye become sensitive to luster variations because luster is one of the most important determinants of value in pearls of all types.

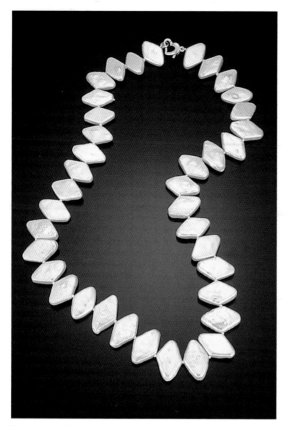

Fig. 11.9 Diamond-shaped cultured Chinese freshwater pearls. They're center drilled widthwise to get a wider necklace and more material per strand. Center drilling them lengthwise would created a longer necklace with less material. *Necklace from Pearlworks; photo by Azad.*

Fig. 11.10 Cultured Chinese freshwater pearls, which are coin-shaped with tails. Top-drilling them is easier and creates a distinctive design. *Necklace from Pearlworks; photo by Azad.*

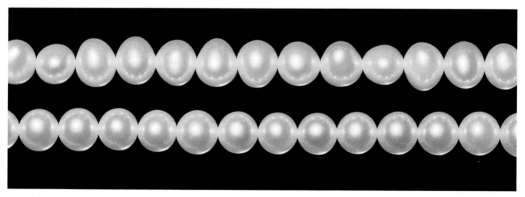

Fig. 11.11 Chinese freshwater strand (top). From a distance it resembles a strand of round saltwater pearls (bottom). Off-round freshwater pearls may sell for 1/3 to 1/10 the price of saltwater pearls of similar luster, size and color depending on their quality category.

Fig. 11.12 Coin and diamond-shaped freshwater pearls with various natural and treated colors. The pearls were cultured in China and are suspended from chain. *Necklace and photo from Shogun Pearl.*

SMOOTHNESS:

The smoother the pearl, the more valuable it is. Even though bumpy, wrinkled surfaces can lower the value of freshwater pearls, the bumps and wrinkles are not considered flaws. Consequently, this chapter treats smoothness as a separate category from surface perfection:

Figure 11.13 shows a close-up view of two qualities of rice pearls. The upper strand is very wrinkled. Therefore, it is worth less than the lower strand with the smoother pearls.

SIZE/WEIGHT:

Freshwater pearl size is not as important of a price factor as is luster and surface quality. Freshwater pearl prices are generally quoted by weight or by the strand. The gram is probably the most common unit of weight used at the retail level, but some dealers quote prices according to carat weight. Suppliers of large quantities of pearls may use the "momme" which equals 3.75 grams (18.75 carats). The measurements of pearls are often listed along with their weight as an additional description and means of identification. The size of round freshwater pearls may be expressed by their diameter, measured in millimeters.

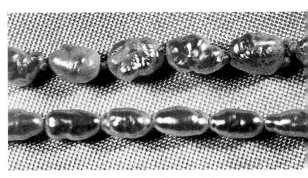

Fig. 11.13 Compare the smoothness of these two strands.

SHAPE:

Usually the more round a pearl is, the greater its value. Good symmetry, too, can make a shape more valuable. In addition, thin shapes tend to sell for less than fatter-looking shapes. Most freshwater pearls are baroque shaped. This is the lowest priced shape, all other factors being equal. Large high-quality, baroque shapes can command high prices and make distinctive jewelry pieces.

Since 1992, a lot of semi-round (off-round) and ovalish freshwater pearls have become available. Sometimes they are described as **potato, corn** and **pea shapes**. These pearls can be used to make impressive looking jewelry pieces that sell for moderate prices. A more close-up view of off-round freshwater pearls is provided in figures 11.11 and 11.14.

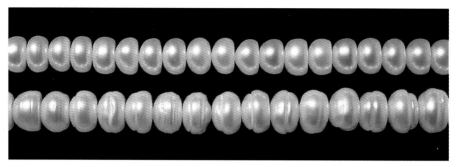

Fig. 11.14 Freshwater pearls that resemble corn kernels

Stick, square, coin, diamond and rectangular shapes are other typical freshwater pearl shapes. Examples are shown in figures 11.12 and 11.15.

Pearl shapes of freshwater and saltwater pearls are determined by a variety of factors:

♦ The type of irritant causing the pearl—mantle tissue, shell bead plus mantle tissue, or in the case of natural pearls parasite or shell piece. Round pearls are more easily cultivated with shell beads or with beads made from tissue-nucleated freshwater pearls. Most freshwater pearl mussels are implanted only with mantle tissue.

♦ The shape of the irritant. Pearl shapes tend to conform to that of the irritant. It's relatively easy to cut mantle tissue in a variety of shapes. This is one of the main reasons freshwater pearls come in so many different shapes which make them ideal for creative jewelry designs.

♦ The length of the cultivation period. Generally the longer the pearl is in the mollusk, the more likely it is to have an irregular shape. With Chinese rice pearls, though, too short of a cultivation period may increase their chances of looking wrinkled and unsymmetrical.

♦ The position of the irritant in the mollusk. If the pearl is in a spot where it can be turned as the mollusk moves around, it may have a greater chance of growing smoothly and symmetrically.

♦ The quality of the irritant. For example, baroque shapes are sometimes the result of flaws in the shell bead nuclei.

♦ The type of mollusk used to culture the pearl. In China, the *sankaku* mussel is more likely to produce a smoother, more round shape than a *kurasu* mussel.

SURFACE QUALITY:

Obvious blemishes such as discolorations, pits and cavities can decrease the value of a pearl considerably, especially if the pearl is otherwise of high quality. Normally, though, flaws in freshwater pearls aren't very noticeable, due to their baroque shapes. Consequently, surface imperfections tend to have less of an effect on the value of freshwater pearls than on those of saltwater pearls.

Fig. 11.15 An array of freshwater pearl shapes. *Pearls and photo from Shogun Pearl.*

Fig. 11.16 One of the first strands of natural color pink freshwater pearls cultured in China (1978) and a neckpiece set with a tourmaline carved by Doug Klein. *Design by Fred & Kate Pearce, photo by Tommy Elder.*

Fig. 11.17 Irradiated and dyed, top-drilled cultured freshwater pearls and amethyst. *Design copyright by Fred and Kate Pearce; photo by Charlie Frieberg.*

COLOR:

Fresh water pearls come in a wide variety of body colors—white, pink, orange, yellow, lavender, gray. Some pearls are even bi-colored. When you ask freshwater pearl dealers what are the most valued body colors, you get a variety of answers. Some price their white pearls higher, others place a higher value on certain colors such as pink and mauve, some raise the prices as the intensity of the colors increases, while other dealers price all the colors about the same. Since the color grading of freshwater pearls is so flexible, the best way to know how an individual pearl dealer prices color is to ask. Most freshwater pearl dealers would agree on the following:

◆ The body color does not affect the price of freshwater pearls as much as it does that of saltwater pearls.
◆ The presence of overtone colors such as pink and silver makes them more valuable.
◆ Iridescence (orient) increases the value of pearls. Iridescence and high luster are interrelated.
◆ Natural color pearls are more highly valued than those which are dyed and/or irradiated. Dark colors are most likely treated, but some factories treat lighter colors in order to strengthen them.

NACRE THICKNESS

Nacre thickness is not as important of a factor in cultured freshwater pearls as it is in saltwater pearls. This is because most freshwater pearls do not have a shell nucleus. When one is present, the nacre is usually thicker than in Akoya pearls. One of the biggest selling points of freshwater pearls is that they usually have a higher percentage of pearl nacre than their saltwater counterparts.

Freshwater pearls typically cost less than saltwater pearls. Low prices, though, don't necessarily mean low quality. Some $20 strands of Chinese freshwater pearls have a better luster, more orient and a higher percentage of pearl nacre than the majority of cultured saltwater pearls on the market today. Therefore, don't just judge pearls by their price tag. Consider their luster, their color, their uniqueness. If you do, you'll discover that freshwater pearls offer great variety, beauty and value.

12

Pearl Treatments

All pearls must be cleaned and washed to remove residue and odors. They are typically tumbled in rotating barrels with salt during this procedure. The tumbling must be closely monitored; otherwise some of the nacre may wear off. There are other processes which are not considered routine and which should therefore be disclosed. Some of these are listed below.

Bleaching: Chinese freshwater pearls and medium-to low-quality Akoya pearls are often bleached with chemicals after drilling. This whitens them and makes the color look more even. Improper bleaching can soften the nacre and make it more susceptible to wear, especially if the nacre is thin. High quality pearls do not need to be bleached, and it would be pointless to possibly reduce their luster and durability by treating them. American freshwater pearls, black pearls and light colored South Sea pearls are not normally bleached. However, this is changing with white South Sea pearls. Some are now undergoing chemical bleaching.

Buffing: This is occasionally done to improve luster and remove superficial scratches. Beeswax or chemical polishes are sometimes used during buffing to add luster. The wax wears off fast and the chemicals may eat away the nacre. Buffing without chemical intervention is considered acceptable if it's done to clean off oil and dirt from the pearl and remove minor scratches.

Coating: There have been reports of pearls being coated with lacquer, but it's difficult to find samples. If pearls were to be coated in this manner, the lacquer would temporarily improve luster. It would eventually wear off over time, leaving buyers feeling deceived if they were not advised of the coating. Good-quality pearls do not have to be coated to look lustrous.

In a few instances, pearls have been darkened with thin plastic coatings to make them look like Tahitian pearls. This coating can be easily detected by its strange feel and by bald spots on the pearl where the coating may have worn away. Coating pearls in this manner is not an accepted trade practice.

Filling: Low-quality cultured baroque pearls are occasionally filled with an epoxy substance if they are partially hollow or have a loose nucleus. This helps the bead nucleus stay in position when the pearls are restrung; it makes the pearls more solid and improves their durability.

"Hollow natural pearls are often filled with foreign materials to bring them to somewhere near the weight one would expect for a pearl of that size," reports Stephen J. Kennedy of the Gem Testing Laboratory of Great Britain. He provided this information with supporting photographs at the AGA Symposium '98 Seminar in Tucson, Arizona and in the January-March 1998 issue of the *Australian Gemmologist*. Natural pearls are often sold by weight. Fillings can be detected with x-radiographs.

Dyeing: White or cream-colored pearls are sometimes soaked in pink dye to give them a desirable pink tint. This dye can often be detected in the drill holes or in cracks (12.1 & 12.2). Yellow and golden pearls may also be dyed (figs 12.3–12.6). These pearls are especially popular in Asia.

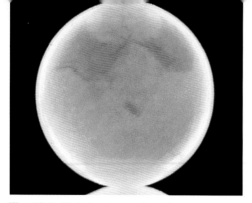

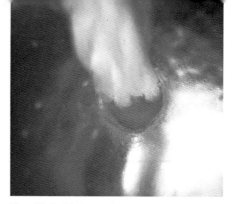

Fig. 12.1 Pink dye in pearl cracks   **Fig. 12.2** Pink dye in pearl drill-hole

Shane Elen of the GIA Research Department has written some excellent articles on how to identify treated and untreated South Sea yellow pearls in *Gems & Gemology*: Summer 2001, Spring 2002 and Summer 2002. In some cases, it can be very difficult and even impossible for gem labs to prove that yellow pearls are of natural color.

Off-color pearls from the Akoya and silver- or gold-lip oysters are sometimes darkened with dye to improve their appearance. Then they are sold as "black pearls." Some of the dark dyes make the pearls look iridescent. If black pearls are smaller than 8 mm, just assume they are dyed Akoya pearls. Dyeing these small pearls is an accepted trade practice because it provides consumers with an option that is not available from natural-color Akoya pearls. Nevertheless, the treatment must be disclosed.

Light-colored pearls from the black-lip oyster are occasionally darkened when there is low demand for very light Tahitian colors. Many people associate the term "dyed" with the terms "cheap" and "fake." However, dyed black pearls were sold in fashionable stores as far back as the 1930's—long before black pearls were being commercially cultivated. Dyed black pearls were considered elegant. They are still in demand. Plus, they have the added bonus of being much more affordable than their naturally-colored counterparts. A large percentage of the pink pearls sold in stores have also been dyed and this means there's a wider selection of pink pearls available for consumers.

If pearls are not properly dyed, the color won't be stable. Therefore it's important to buy dyed pearls from reputable jewelers. That way if there is a problem, you'll be able to return the pearls and get a refund. If you're buying expensive *untreated* pearls, have them checked by an independent gem laboratory. Some are listed on page 110 at the end of the Chapter 14.

In recent years, there has been a problem of nacre peeling off of dyed Akoya pearls with thin nacre. On dark pearls, chipped nacre can be quite noticeable and unattractive. As a result, some dealers have stopped selling dyed Akoyas to avoid the hassle of returns and customer complaints.

Irradiation: This method works best on freshwater pearls, but off-color Akoya and South Sea pearls may also be darkened in this manner. It involves bombarding pearls with gamma rays. This blackens the shell bead nucleus of Akoya and South Sea pearls and can make their nacre appear dark if it is thin. Sometimes pearls are both dyed and irradiated. The irradiation will give them an iridescent bluish or greenish gray color and the dye will further darken their appearance.

Silver salt treatment: This is the most common way of blackening Akoya pearls. The pearls are soaked in a weak solution of silver nitrate and diluted ammonia and then exposed to light or hydrogen sulfide gas. Unfortunately, the silver nitrate tends to weaken pearls and make them more susceptible to wear. Silver nitrate treatments can usually be detected by X-radiography.

Dying the bead nucleus: Occasionally shell bead nuclei are dyed before they are inserted in the oyster. Afterwards the dark bead may show through the nacre and make the pearl nacre look dark.

Fig. 12.3 A strand of low-quality dyed South Sea pearls

Fig. 12.4 Visible dye concentrations

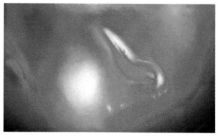

Fig. 12.5 Magnified view of a blemish in one of the dyed pearls in figure 12.3

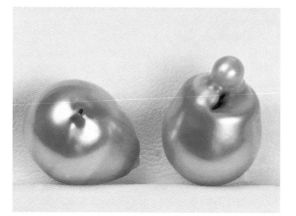

Fig. 12.6 Dye concentrations and black nucleus visible in blemishes of two dyed pearls

Fig. 12.7 Dyed and/or irradiated freshwater pearls

Natural Color or Not?

As you can see, dyeing is not the only means of coloring pearls. However, for the sake of brevity, the term "**dyed**" will be used in the rest of this chapter to describe any artificially colored pearl.

Dyed pearls are not fakes, but they are normally considered less valuable than those of natural color. There is an especially large price difference between true black or golden South Sea pearls and those which aren't, so you should know how to protect yourself from being charged a natural-color pearl price for a dyed pearl. Even if the price is fair, you may just prefer pearls of natural color. You can reduce your chances of being misled with the following tests:

Price Test   Is the price unusually low compared to natural-color pearls of the same size, shape and overall quality? An nice-quality, round, 8-mm natural-color black or gold pearl can retail for between $150 to $300. A round, 8-mm dyed pearl may retail for about $40 to $100. (Remember to compare pearls of the same size and shape. These factors have a major effect on the price. For example, if we just decreased the size of the dyed pearl to 6 mm, it could retail for about $20.)

True black pearls are typically expensive, so if the price is low and you're not in Tahiti, assume the pearl is dyed unless otherwise told. (It's illegal to import or sell dyed black pearls in Tahiti.) Keep in mind, however, that good quality dyed pearls are not cheap.

Dyed golden pearls can be sold anywhere so always ask if the color is natural. If the store claims the color is natural, ask if they will write this on the receipt.

Size Test   Is the size less than 8 mm? If so, and you are not in Tahiti, assume that it is an Akoya dyed pearl or an Akoya "blue pearl" (a dark colored pearl which derives its color from foreign contaminants in the nacre itself or between the nacre and the shell bead nucleus). There are true black Tahitian pearls less than 8 mm, but it is usually not cost effective to intentionally produce them when farmers can get far more by cultivating larger pearls. If a dark pearl is of natural color, the store should be willing to write this on the receipt.

Akoya oysters, on the other hand, can produce a wide range of pearls below 9 mm; but rarely do they grow round pearls above 10 mm. Larger Japanese baroque pearls may be available. A photo of some Japanese "blue pearls" ranging from 11.5–14 mm can be seen in the fall 1990 issue of *Gems & Gemology* (p. 225).

Once in a while, large round pearls from South Sea oysters are dyed or are "blue pearls." Therefore large size is never proof that a pearl is a true black pearl. It is, however, a positive sign. When buying black pearls, it's advisable to ask salespeople to specify on the receipt that the pearls are of natural color. When spending large sums of money, also have them tested by an independent gem lab.

Drill-hole Test   If it's possible to look into the drill hole with a loupe, does the nacre inside look white and the nucleus look dark? This is a sign the pearl has been colored by irradiation or the nucleus has been dyed. Is there dye concentrated around the drill hole? This indicates it's dyed.

Sometimes undrilled dyed golden pearls have pits or cracks which allow you to see a dark nucleus (fig. 12.6).

Fig. 12.8 Tahitian black pearl solitaire of natural color and a smaller black, dyed Akoya pearl. Assume that black pearls less than 8 mm are dyed and/or irradiated. *Jewelry by Erica Courtney; photo by Ralph Gabriner.*

Fig. 12.9 Japanese Akoya pearls. Top to bottom: dyed black, gray (non-natural color), light blue (natural color), and dyed blue.

Color Test

Are the pearls so dark they're almost black or so yellow they look fake? Do all the pearls in the piece look the exact same color? Is the color perfectly even in all the pearls? Do the yellow or gold pearls look grayish? These are indications the pearls might be dyed. It's not easy to find several black or yellow pearls the exact same even color. Neither is it easy to find true black pearls that are really black. More often than not they are grayish.

If you're interested in black pearls, look at a lot of them. Then look at dyed pearls and compare. Gradually, you'll get a sense of what

Fig. 12.10 Natural-color golden pearls with normal color variation. *Pendant & earrings from Divina Pearls; photo, Cristina Gregory.*

the body colors and overtones of black pearls look like. People who work with black or yellow pearls on a regular basis can usually spot dyed pearls instantly. But even experts can be fooled. So when making a major purchase, have your pearls tested by an independent gem lab.

Magnifier Test
Examine the surface of the pearl with a 10-power magnifier (loupe). If the color in or around the blemishes is stronger and more intense than the rest of the pearl, this is a good sign the pearl is dyed. After dealers examine sample dyed pearls in this manner, they can easily detect dye concentrations when blemishes are present. Absence of visible dye is not proof of natural color; not all blemishes of dyed pearls show dye.

Many appraisers, jewelers and gemology students use this book as a reference, and they're interested in some of the more technical ways of detecting dyed pearls. The following methods require special equipment and are not cost effective for the consumer. Nevertheless, some lay people are interested in tests which gem labs may conduct:

Infrared Test If you have a camera, you can photograph the pearls with color infrared film(Kodak, Ektachrome Infrared Film, IE 135-20). Naturally colored pearls tend to look blue, whereas pearls colored with silver salts generally look yellow (or range from greenish blue to yellow green). (Komatsu and Akamatsu, *Gems & Gemology*, Spring 1978).

Fiberoptic Test If black pearls appear brownish under fiberoptic illumination but not under tungsten light-bulbs, this suggests they were dyed with silver nitrate. Good quality, natural-color Tahitian pearls usually retain their normal colors under fiberoptic lights. Occasionally, low-grade, mottled Tahitian pearls look brownish. (Stephen Kennedy, *Australian Gemmologist*, January-March 1998, p.18.)

Fluorescence The pearls are examined under long-wave UV radiation. Natural-color black pearls will generally have a fluorescence ranging from a bright red (pearls from Baja California) to a dull reddish brown (Tahitian pearls). Dyed pearls tend to show no reaction or else fluoresce a dull green. (See page 143 of the 1989 issue of *Gems & Gemology*, part of a good article on the Polynesian black pearl by Marisa Goebel and Dona Dirlam.)

Microscope The pearls are viewed under a 100+-power microscope through crossed Polaroid lenses. Traces of the chemical coloring can be seen. (Hisada and Komatsu, *Pearls of the World,* pp. 92-93).

X-radiograph An x-ray photo called an **x-radiograph** is taken of the pearls. If the pearls are dyed with silver salts, a pale ring between the nacre and the shell bead nucleus can often be seen. In addition, there is less of a contrast between the bead and the nacre.

X-ray Fluorescence The pearls are exposed to x-rays. Then the emitted wavelengths are measured with an instru-ent called a spectrometer to detect trace elements such as silver on the surface of the pearl.

As you can see, there is a wide variety of tests for identifying dyed pearls. Use a combination of the simple tests to help you spot obvious cases of dye. But when it comes to making a major purchase, get help from professionals.

Fig. 12.11 Dyed freshwater pearls. *Lariat & photo by Angela Conty.*

13

Imitation or Not?

Imagine a rosary-bead maker watching a fish being scaled in a basin of water. The water has colorful, pearly reflections which seem to form as the fish scales dissolve. The bead maker then gets the idea to filter the water, recover the pearly substance from it and mix it with a kind of varnish. Later he coats the inside surface of a hollow glass bead with the pearly mixture, fills the bead with wax, and what's the result? The birth of the modern-day imitation pearl.

This occurred in France in the 17th century. Jacquin was the name of the rosary-bead maker. And **essence of orient** (or **pearl essence**) is the name of the pearly mixture he discovered. Today, the finest imitation pearls usually have several coats of essence of orient.

Types of Imitation Pearls

Even though pearl essence is used to make many of the best imitation pearls, such as Majorica pearls. Imitations come in a variety of types. The main ones are:

♦ **Hollow glass beads containing wax**. These pearls, made by the same process as Jacquin's, are most likely to be found in antique jewelry.

♦ **Solid glass beads**. Majorica imitation pearls are an example of this type. They may be covered with as many as forty coats of pearl essence and hand polished between each coat. Imitation glass pearls are also coated with other substances such as synthetic pearl essence, plastic, cellulose and lacquer.

♦ **Plastic beads**. These may have the same type coatings as the glass type. Plastic imitation pearl necklaces sometimes hang poorly due to their light weight.

♦ **Mother-of-pearl shell beads.** These are coated with the same substances as plastic and glass imitations. A coating made from powdered mother of pearl and synthetic resin may also be used. One company calls such beads **semi-cultured**. This is just a misleading term for "imitation." Powdered mother-of-pearl coatings are not new. Centuries ago, American Indians produced imitation pearls by applying such coatings to clay beads and then baking them.

Occasionally, people sell uncoated mother-of-pearl beads as pearls or they describe them as very valuable. In the Pacific Islands, you can buy mother-of-pearl shell bead necklaces from the natives for a couple of dollars. Some of the better ones cost more.

Simulated and **faux pearls** (the French term for fake pearls) are two other terms used to designate imitation pearls. These pearls can be distinguished from natural and cultured pearls with the following tests.

Tests that Require No Equipment Other Than a Magnifier

Tooth Test

Rub the pearls **lightly** along the biting edge of your upper front teeth. If they feel gritty or sandy, it's likely they are cultured or natural pearls. If they feel smooth, they are probably imitations.

There are a few problems with this test. It's not the most sanitary test. It may scratch the pearls, if done improperly. And it doesn't always work. There are some imitation pearls that feel gritty. Also, according to the Fall 1991 issue of *Gems & Gemology* (p. 176), real pearls may feel smooth. A cultured pearl sent to the GIA New York laboratory gave a smooth tooth test reaction because the surface had been polished. Therefore, don't rely solely on the tooth test. If you use it, combine it with the magnification tests listed below.

Surface Magnification

Examine the surface of the pearl with a 10-power magnifier such as a loupe. If it looks grainy, like a photo taken at an ISO of 1000 and above, there's a good chance it's an imitation (fig. 13.1). Pearls normally look unusually fine grained. Sometimes, though, dirt or pits on a pearl may make it seem to have a grainy appearance. Occasionally, too, freshwater and South Sea pearls may look a little grainy, but other surface characteristics mentioned in this section can prove they are not imitation.

If you have access to a microscope, also examine the surface at the highest possible magnification. At 50 power and above, a rough, pitted surface like the one in figure 13.2 means it's an imitation. Gas bubbles may also be present.

A surface with tiny, crooked lines giving it a scaly, maze-like appearance is characteristic of cultured and natural pearls (fig. 13.4). These scaly lines are not always evident at first. The surface may look smooth except for the flaws. Try using a strong, bare, direct light such as a fiber-optic; and shine it on the pearl from various angles to find the scaly lines. It's curious that pearls, which feel gritty to the teeth, can look so smooth under high magnification; whereas imitations, which feel smooth, tend to look coarse and rough. However, the less smooth an imitation is, the rougher it looks. On pearls, it's the "scaly-line" ridges that cause their gritty feel.

Fig. 13.1 Grainy surface texture of an imitation pearl viewed at 10-power magnification.

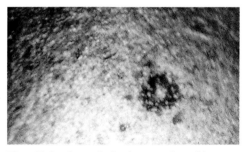

Fig. 13.2 Same imitation pearl at 64-power magnification. Note the rough surface.

Fig 13.3 Under 10X magnification, the surface of the imitation pearl (top) looks coarse and grainy compared to the smoother-looking surface of the real cultured pearl (bottom).

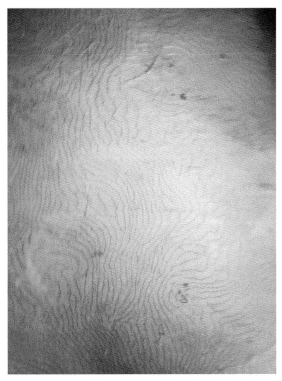

Fig. 13.4 Surface of a Tahitian cultured pearl viewed at 64-power magnification. The maze-like patterns prove the pearl is genuine. When rubbed lightly against the biting edge of the front teeth, the pearl feels gritty due to the microscopic surface ridges.

The best way to learn what the surface of pearls and imitations looks like under magnification is to examine many examples of each. When you can recognize how distinctive their surface textures are, you won't need to do any of the other tests to spot an imitation pearl.

Flaw Test

Examine the pearls for flaws. If they appear flawless, this is a sign they're imitation. Also note the types of flaws present. Many of those found on cultured pearls look different from those on imitations. If you examine pearl flaws with a 10-power magnifier whenever possible, it will be easier for you to recognize them. Chapter 6 shows examples of pearl flaws.

Matching Test

Note the shape, luster, size and color of the pearls. Imitations often seem perfectly matched, whereas there tend to be variations among the pearls on cultured or natural strands.

Heaviness Test

Bounce the pearls in your hand. If they feel unusually light, they're most likely made of plastic or filled with wax. Solid glass beads may feel heavier or about the same as cultured and natural pearls.

Fig. 13.5 Top two strands—cultured pearls, bottom strand—good-quality imitation pearls. Genuine pearls of good quality will typically have either pink, green, silver or blue overtones; whereas imitations tend to lack these overtones and be more uniform in color. A better way of distinguishing imitation from genuine pearls is to examine them with a 10-power magnifier.

Overtone Test

Look for overtone colors in the pearls. Imitations frequently have none, and when they do, the overtones all tend to look the same. It's normal for cultured and natural pearls to have overtones, and these overtones often vary in color within the strand (fig. 13.5).

Drill Hole Test

Examine the drill hole area with a magnifier of 10-power or above. (On some pearls, it may be hard to see into their drill hole.) Cultured pearls tend to show the following characteristics (figs. 13.6–13.9):
- There is often a clear dividing line between the nacre and nucleus.
- The edges of the drill holes are often sharp and well defined. But when the nacre wears away it can leave the holes looking jagged and rough as in figures 13.8 and 13.9.
- The drill holes tend to be like a straight cylinder.
- The pearl nacre coating is normally thicker than the coating of imitations.

Imitation pearls tend to show these characteristics (figs 13.10 & 13.11):
- There is normally no dark dividing line between the coating and the rest of the pearl. Occasionally, one may see a kind of line, but the other characteristics of the drill hole will look like those of imitations. If you are in doubt, look at the drill hole opening on the other side of the pearl and on other pearls of the strand.
- The coating around the edges of the drill holes may have flaked off, making it look ragged or uneven.
- The drill holes may be angled outward at the surface of the pearl. Other times the drill holes may round inward at the surface and bow outward inside the pearl.
- The coating often looks like a thin coat of shiny paint. The thinness can be seen at the edge of the drill hole or around bare areas which expose the inner bead.
- Rounded ridges may have formed around the drill hole.
- If the bead is made of glass, its glassy luster may be apparent.

100

Drill Holes of Cultured Pearls

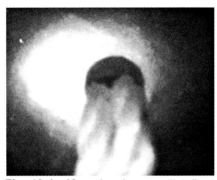

Fig. 13.6 Note the sharp, well-defined edges of the drill hole. The line between the nacre and nucleus is hard to see due to the thickness of the nacre.

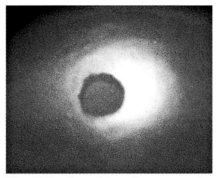

Fig. 13.7 A straight drill hole and the separation line between the core and thin nacre indicate this is a cultured pearl.

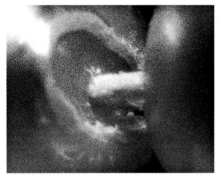

Fig. 13.8 The coating of both cultured and imitation pearls can wear way at the drill hole, but pearl nacre has a distinctive appearance and is usually thicker than that of imitations.

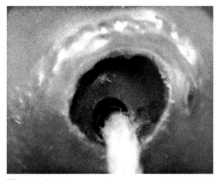

Fig. 13.9 The nacre has separated from the core in this pearl. A separation like this would not be characteristic of an imitation pearl.

Drill Holes of Imitation Pearls

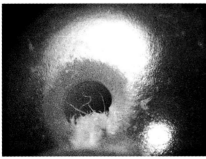

Fig. 13.10 The very thin ragged coating, angled-in drill hole, and lack of dividing line between core and coating indicate this is an imitation.

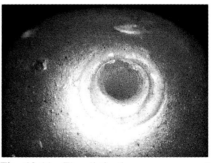

Fig. 13.11 The distinctive appearance of the coating, lack of dividing line, and the drill-hole which bows outward inside (not visible in photo) mean this is an imitation.

Clasp Test   Is the clasp made of silver, steel or a gold plated metal. This is a warning sign that the strand may be imitation. But good pearls are occasionally strung with cheap clasps and imitation ones with expensive clasps.

Price Test   Is the price of the pearls unbelievably low? If so, they may be imitation or have hardly any pearl nacre. Jewelers can't stay in business if they sell pearls below their cost.

Other Tests

X-radiograph Test   An x-ray photo called an **x-radiograph** is taken of the pearls. Imitations are opaque to x-rays making them look solid white on the negative and solid black on the positive print made of it. Cultured and natural pearls are semitransparent to x-rays and usually look grayish.

Since imitations pearls can be positively identified with other tests, x-raying them is usually a waste of money. There is, however, a major advantage to the x-ray test. It's quicker to x-ray an entire strand at once than to test each pearl in it individually.

Refractometer Test   The "pearl" is placed on a refractometer (an instrument that measures a gem's **refractive index**—the degree to which light is bent as it passes through the gem). A pearl will generally have a low reading of 1.530 and a high one of 1.685. The numerical difference between these two readings is .155 and is called its **birefringence**. Pearls have an unusually high birefringence compared to other gems. This causes a blinking and pink effect when their refractive index is read through a rotating Polaroid filter. The GIA Pearls Course states that the presence of this "birefringent blink" is proof a pearl is not an imitation.

The refractive index of some imitations can also prove they are not cultured or natural pearls. For example, the Majorica imitation pearls the GIA tested for their Fall 1990 article in *Gems and Gemology* had a refractive index of 1.48, which was a conclusive means of identification.

Distinguishing between imitations and pearls is not hard. Even lay people can learn how to detect imitations with a loupe, but they do need practice. What's hard is to distinguish cultured pearls from those that are natural. This will be the focus of the next chapter.

14

Natural or Cultured?

In 1917, Cartier bought their building in New York with two strands of natural pearls valued at a million dollars. In 1957, the pearls were sold at auction for $157,000. Perhaps one of the main reasons for this drop in price, was the introduction of the cultured pearl, which decreased the demand for natural pearls.

Prices of natural pearls have risen considerably since 1957, but they still don't match those of the early 1900's. Nevertheless, natural pearls are still worth a lot more than cultured pearls. Therefore, it's important to be able to distinguish between them. X-ray tests are generally required to prove a pearl is natural, but they are costly. Other tests can help you determine a pearl is cultured and thereby save you the expense of an x-ray. These tests are listed below. Keep in mind that almost all the pearls produced today are cultured. You are most likely to find natural pearls in antique pieces. (Whole pearls were not cultured before the 1900's.) However, the natural pearls in antique jewelry may have been replaced with cultured ones.

Tests a Layperson Can Do

Drill Hole Test

Look inside the drill hole with a 10-power magnifier. If you can see a dark dividing line separating the nacre from a pearl bead nucleus, the pearl is cultured. This dark line is conchiolin, the material which binds the nacre to the bead. Natural pearls may show a series of growth lines, which get more yellow or brown towards the center of the pearl. A black deposit at the center of a white pearl can be a sure sign the pearl is natural.(From *Gem Testing* by B. W. Anderson, page 219.)

Also note the size of the drill hole. The drill holes of natural pearls are rarely larger than .04 mm (.016 inch). Those of cultured pearls tend to measure .06 mm (.024 inch). (From *Pearls* by Jean Taburiaux, page 193.) Natural pearls are partly valued by weight, so the holes are made as small as possible to minimize weight loss.

Shape Test

Do the pearls look perfectly round? If so, then it's likely they're cultured. Natural pearls tend to have at least slightly irregular shapes, even though a few are round. This test is only an indication. It is not proof

Blink Test

Hold the strand near the front edge of a strong desk lamp. The light should shine through the pearls but not in your eyes. Rotate the strand. If the pearls blink from light to dark as they are turned, this indicates they are cultured and have a thin coating of nacre (imitation pearls with mother-of-pearl shell-bead centers may also blink). The dark areas result when there are dense mother-

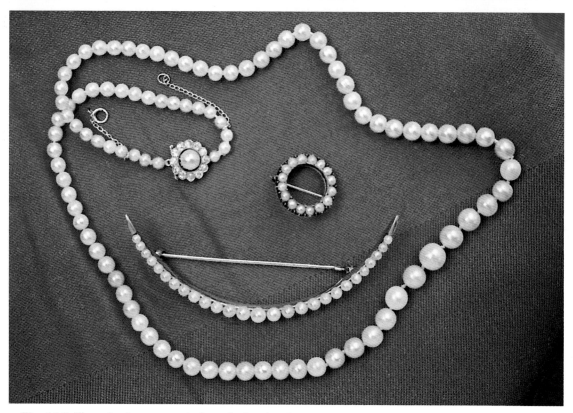

Fig. 14.1 Natural saltwater pearls from the Persian Gulf and the coast of Central Asia (Oriental pearls). *Jewelry and photograph from the collection of K. C. Bell.*

Fig. 14.2 Hand-executed Ceylonese gold neckpiece bead-set with natural pearls from Ceylon (Sri Lanka), early 19th century from the collection of K.C. Bell. *Photo by K.C. Bell.*

Fig. 14.3 Natural saltwater pearl cross (17th century) from Venezuela. K. C. Bell, the importer and photographer of these pearls, refers to them as "Occidental Pearls."

104

Fig. 14.4 Natural abalone pearls from the coast of Baja California. *Earrings by Eve Alfillé; photo, Matthew Arden.*

Fig. 14.5 Natural American freshwater pearls and pink cultured semi-round pearls. *Pin/clasp, necklace and photo by Angela Conty*

of-pearl layers on the shell bead which block the light. Figure 14.6 shows light and dark views of thin-nacre pearls with transmitted light. Cultured pearls with thin nacre may show only one view when rotated. In other words, they don't necessarily blink.

Stripe Test

As you rotate the pearls with strong light shining through them, look for curved lines and stripes (fig. 14.6). These are the growth layers of the shell beads. If they are visible, the nacre is very thin and the pearls are cultured. Not all shell bead nuclei show stripes, though. This can be seen in figure 14.7. Keep in mind that imitation pearls with shell-bead centers can also display this banded effect. Natural pearls, however, will not look striped.

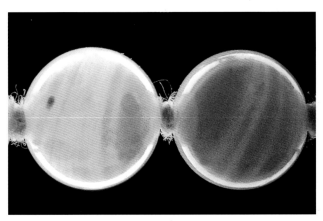

Fig. 14.6 Dark and light views of thin-nacre pearls in transmitted light. Note the curved bands which indicate the growth layers of the shell bead nucleus.

105

Fig. 14.7 Mother-of-pearl shell beads (the core of cultured pearls) seen with transmitted light

Color Test   Examine the color. Cultured pearls often have a faint greenish tint, unlike natural pearls. Some dealers find that the color of natural pearls has a greater potential for brightness than that of cultured pearls. Color can only suggest a pearl might be cultured. It is not proof.

Matching Test   Because of their rarity, it's difficult to find natural pearls that match. Consequently, natural strands do not appear as well matched for color, shape, luster and size as those which are cultured.

Other Tests

X-radiograph Test   This is the most reliable way to distinguish between natural and cultured pearls. On an x-radiograph negative, cultured pearls usually show a clear separation between core and nacre. Plus, their core normally looks lighter than the nacre coating. X-rayed natural pearls tend to either look the same tone throughout or get darker in their center. A mantle tissue nucleus will look like a very dark, irregular-shaped void.

   The disadvantage of x-ray tests is that it can cost between $100 and $300 to have them done, and there are few gem labs that have the required equipment. Stephen J. Kennedy of the Gem Testing Laboratory of Great Britian provides good photos of x-radiographs in an article entitled "Pearl Identification" in the January-March 1998 issue of the Australian Gemmologist. This is also an excellent source of additional information on the identification of natural pearls.

X-ray Fluorescence   This test is used in combination with an x-radiograph to provide the added information of whether the pearl is freshwater or saltwater. Natural saltwater pearls rarely fluoresce to x-rays. Freshwater pearls have a fairly strong yellowish x-ray fluorescence, whereas bead-nucleated salt-water pearls

Fig. 14.8 Natural pearls of various shapes, colors and sizes. *Photo and pearls courtesy Mikimoto (America) Ltd.*

display a greenish fluorescence Cultured pearls dyed with silver salts usually show no fluorescence.

Specific Gravity Test The pearls are placed in a liquid that has a specific gravity of 2.71 (purchased at gem instrument stores and tested with a piece of pure calcite). The majority of natural pearls will float and others will sink slowly. Most cultured pearls with shell nuclei will sink quickly since they tend to be heavier than natural pearls. Black pearls show an SG of about 2.65. The biggest problem with this test is that the heavy liquid may damage the pearls, especially if the pearls are left in it too long. (See *Identification of Gemstones* by Michael O'Donoghue and Louise Joyner).

UV Fluorescence Test The pearls are placed under long-wave ultraviolet light and compared to known samples of cultured and natural pearls. In his book *Gemstones* (p. 448), G. F. Herbert Smith mentions how cultured pearls can display a peculiar greenish fluorescence which differs markedly from the sky-blue effect of many natural pearls. He points out that this is not an infallible test because natural pearls can also have a greenish fluorescence, particularly if they are from waters adjacent to those of cultured pearls. Consequently, gem labs with x-ray equipment do not use this test. However, this test may help those without x-ray machines. Seeing a unique sky-blue fluorescence under LW UV light instead of a greenish-yellow glow may serve as an additional incentive to pay for an x-ray to test for natural origin. (This test is also mentioned in Webster' *Gems* on page 539.) Cultured pearl strands tend to show greater uniformity in the intensity of color.

107

If the pearls are of good quality and preliminary tests suggest they may be natural, then it's advisable to have them x-rayed. Appraisers and jewelers can send them to the appropriate labs for you. Some of the gem labs that have the facilities to do x-ray tests are listed below. Jewelers in your area may know of others.

AGTA Gemological Testing Center
18 E. 48th Street, Suite 502
New York, NY 10017
(212) 752-1717, Fax 750-0930
e-mail info@agta-gtc.org

AIGS (Asian Institute of Gem Sciences)
919/1 Jewelry Trade Center, 33rd floor
Bangrak, Bangkok, 10500, Thailand
(66-2) 267-4315- (66-2) 267-4320
www.aigsthailand.com

Central Gem Laboratory
5-15-14 Ueno 5-Chome
Taito-ku, Tokyo 110-0005, Japan
(81) 3 (3836) 3219, Fax 3832-6861

CISGEM
Via della Ordole, 4,1-20123
Milan, Italy
39 02 8515 5230, Fax 8515-5258

DSEF (German Gemmolgical Laboratory)
Prof-Schlossmacher-Str. 1
D-55743 Idar-Oberstein, Germany
49 6781-43011, Fax 49 6781-41616
www.gemcertificate.com

Gem Testing Laboratory of Great Britain
27 Greville Street (Saffron Hill Entrance)
London EC1N8TN
Tel. (44) (207) 405-3351, Fax 831-9479
www.gem-a.info or www.gagtl.ac.uk

Gem Sciences International
P.O. Box 430
Deer Park, CA 94576-0430
(707) 968-0636

GIA Gem Trade Laboratory, Inc.
5345 Armada Drive
Carlsbad, CA 92008
Tel. (800) 421-7250 & (760) 603-4500
www.gia.org
or
580 Fifth Ave.
New York, NY 10036
Tel. (212) 221-5858

Gubelin Gemmological Laboratory
Maihofstrasse 102
6006 Lucerne, Switzerland
Tel. (41) (41) 26 17 17
www.gubelinlab.com

Laboratoire Francaise de Gemmologie
2 Place de la Bourse
75002 Paris, France
33- 1- 40262646

SSEF Swiss Gemmological Institute
Falknerstrasse 9
CH-4001 Basel, Switzerland
Tel. (41) (6) 262-0640 Fax: 262-0641
www.ssef.ch

15

Choosing the Clasp

Mrs. Kirk was proud of the beautiful pearl necklace her daughter had given her, but she hardly ever wore it. She had arthritis, and that made it hard for her to fasten and undo the clasp. Since she lived by herself, nobody was around to help her put on the necklace, so it was easier to leave it in her jewelry box.

Mrs. Kirk is not alone. Complicated or hard-to-fasten clasps keep a lot of people from wearing some of their jewelry pieces. This could be prevented with a bit of forethought. When choosing a clasp, consider:

♦ How secure is it?
♦ How easy is it to open?
♦ How versatile is it?
♦ How much does it cost?

Determine what is most important to you about the clasp because normally, some compromises will have to be made. For example, to get a clasp that is easy to open, you may have to accept less security.

Listed below are four basic pearl clasps along with their advantages and disadvantages.

♦ **Fish-hook clasp** (fig 15.1): This is a popular clasp because it's inexpensive and secure. It may be silver, gold or gold-plated. The main drawback of the fish-hook clasp is that it can be hard to fasten and undo, especially for someone with arthritis or other hand problems.

♦ **Push clasp** (fig. 15.2): The main advantage of this clasp, is that it is fairly easy to open, even with one hand when it's used on a bracelet. It's also relatively inexpensive. Unfortunately, it is not as secure as some of the other clasps.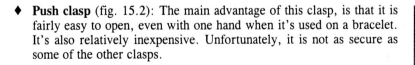

♦ **Lobster clasp** or **lobster claw** (fig. 15.3). Secure, easy to open and relatively inexpensive, this is an ideal clasp both for pearls and gold chains. It's not used as frequently for pearls, however, as the fish clasp and push clasp. If you're having pearls strung, you may wish to request this clasp.

Fig. 15.5 A hinged clasp, which is trademarked **Applaudere** by A & Z Pearls.

Fig. 15.6 Another view of the Applaudere clasp. *Photo by Richard Rubins.*

♦ The screw clasp (fig. 15.4): This clasp can add versatility when it's inserted in pearls to form a **hidden or mystery clasp**. For example, a long strand of pearls with three mystery clasps can be unscrewed and turned into a bracelet and two smaller necklaces.

Fig. 15.4 Mystery clasp

Mystery clasps are fairly easy to open and close and are secure, if they're screwed in all the way and aren't stripped out. They tend to cost a little more than the fish-hook, lobster and push clasps.

Sometimes the string breaks on necklaces with mystery clasps. This can happen when people unscrew the clasp incorrectly or when they can't find the clasp and try to unscrew the necklace in a spot where there is no clasp. This problem can be avoided by having the jeweler show you how to find and open the clasp. When undoing it, be sure to grasp at least two pearls on either side of the clasp. Turn them together as a unit. Don't twist the string.

There are a wide variety of clasps besides these four basic ones. Figures 15.5 & 15.6 show a type of hanged clasp, the Applaudere by A & Z Pearls. Each end of the strand is attached to a clasp. The pair of clasps can be fastened over any of the pearls on the necklace allowing a variety of styles from a single strand of pearls.

Figures 15.8–15.11 show variations of the push clasp. Many clasps are jewelry pieces by themselves and are best worn to the side or in the front of necklaces or on the top of bracelets.

Fig. 15.7 Double ring clasp. *Pearl necklace and photo from Inter World Trading.*

Fig. 15.8 Push clasps set with sapphires, emeralds and pearls. *Photo and clasps from Inter World Trading.*

110

Fig 15.9 Push clasp

Fig. 15.10 Push clasp.

Fig. 15.11 Push clasp

Fig. 15.12 Bar clasp

Fig. 15.13 Push clasp

Fig. 15.14 Foldover clasp

Figs. 15.9–15.14 An array of bracelet clasps from Divina Pearls. *Photo by Cristina Gregory*

Fig. 15.15 Black pearl enhancer suspended from a pink freshwater pearl necklace by Divina Pearls. *Photo by the designer, Cristina Gregory.*

Sometimes accessories are used to accent pearls with plain clasps. One of the most popular pearl accessories is the **pearl enhancer**. It is a pendant which can be attached to a strand of pearls, as well to as a gold chain or bead necklace. The top of the pearl enhancer has a hinged clasp which closes over the necklace between two pearls (figs. 15.15 & 15.16). Centerpieces can be used to create impressive-looking necklaces (figs. 15.17, 15.19, & 15.21).

With the **pin pearl adaptor** (fig 15.20), a pin can be attached to two strands to look like a decorative clasp or it can be worn as a pearl shortener. The pin pearl adaptor slides on to any pin and then can be closed over two strands of pearls.

There are many other types and styles of clasps besides the ones pictured in this chapter. You can see them on display in jewelry stores. No matter what type you choose, do not take a necklace or bracelet home without first having the salesperson show you how to fasten and unfasten the clasp. Then try doing it at least two times by yourself. Some clasps are like puzzles, and if you try to figure them out on your own, you could damage the clasp and/or the pearls.

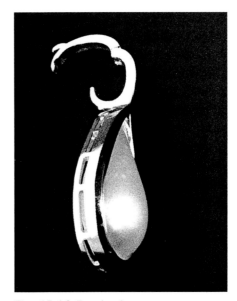

Fig. 15.16 Pearl enhancer

If your budget is limited, put your money into the pearls first, rather than into a fancy clasp. You can always upgrade the clasp later on. When buying a pearl necklace, your first priority should be the pearls.

Fig. 15.17 A centerpiece of 22K and 18K gold, woven by hand by Barbara Berk, and 8 strands of 3 mm dyed Chinese freshwater pearls. *Photo by Dana Davis.*

Fig. 15.18 A diamond bar joining the loose ends of the strands of a tassle necklace by Divina Pearls. *Photo by Christina Gregory.*

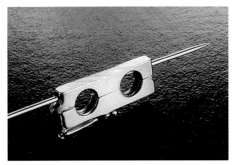

Fig. 15.20 Pin pearl adapter

Fig. 15.19 Antique cameo center-plate and cultured dyed Akoya pearl necklace from Divina Pearls. *Photo by Cristina Gregory.*

Fig. 15.21 Antique platinum old-cut diamond & rubellite center-plate suspended by Divina Pearls. *Photo by Cristina Gregory.*

Fig. 16.a A lariat-style (open-end) cultured akoya pearl necklace. It's knotted and has faceted amethysts at the end. *Designed and photographed by Cristina Gregory of www.DivinaPearls.com.*

Fig. 16.b An antique style necklace made with three strands of dyed black freshwater pearls. *Designed and photographed by Cristina Gregory of www.DivinaPearls.com.*

16

Versatile Ways to Wear a Strand of Pearls

There are no other gems that offer more versatility than pearls. Queen Elizabeth I of England made the most of this feature. She wore yards of them as necklaces hanging down as far her knees. She had them threaded in her wigs, embroidered in her clothing, and set in her crown and other regal jewelry. You can also enjoy the versatility of pearls. The styles listed below and shown in figures 16.1–16.15 can be made with just one opera-length necklace (about 28 to 34 inches) and a pair of hinged clasps like the Applaudere, pictured in figure 15.5 of the previous chapter.

♦ A single strand of adjustable lengths with the clasp in the back (fig. 16.1)
♦ A double strand on one side and single on the other (fig. 16.2)
♦ A double strand choker or princess necklace (fig. 16.3)
♦ A single strand clasped to form one "chain" hanging in the front. (fig. 16.4). An opera-length strand can be worn as a belt in the same manner.
♦ A single strand tied or knotted in front to form two "chains" hanging in the front (fig. 16.5)
♦ Double strand in back and triple strand in the front (fig. 16.6)
♦ A single strand looped in the front with a pearl shortener (fig. 16.7)
♦ Double strand in front and single strand in back (fig. 16.8)
♦ Double strand looped together in front (fig. 16.9)
♦ Single strand with a clasp to the side or in the center (fig. 16.10)
♦ Single strand knotted in the front (fig. 16.11). Dresses with low V-backs can be accented with a rope-length strand tied like this in the back.
♦ Double strand twisted and clasped in the back (fig. 16.12)
♦ Double strand with a loop hanging in the front like a pendant (fig. 16.13)
♦ Double or single strand with a pearl enhancer (detachable pendant) (fig. 16.14)
♦ A closed double strand joined in the front with a solid surface pin.
   (This idea is from Joy's Antique Jewelry in Pittsburgh, PA, fig 16.c)
♦ Multi-strand bracelet (fig. 16.15)
♦ Wrapped in the hair around a chignon or ponytail (fig. 16.16)
♦ Attached to the side with a pin and hanging asymmetrically
♦ Pinned across a V-back dress or sweater

Other options are possible with longer or multi-piece necklaces.
♦ Attached to the shoulders of a dress
♦ Wrapped around a hat
♦ Looped through button-holes or openings in clothing (fig. 16.18)
    These are only some of the ways pearls can be worn. Use your imagination and you'll discover many more.

Fig. 16.c

Fig. 16.1

Fig. 16.2

Fig. 16.3

Fig. 16.4

Fig. 16.5

Fig. 16.6

Fig. 16.7

Fig. 16.8

Fig. 16.9

Fig. 16.10

Fig. 16.11

Fig. 16.12

Fig. 16.13

Fig. 16.14

120

Fig. 16.15

Fig. 16.16 Photo courtesy of the Cultured Pearl Associations of America & Japan

Fig. 16.17 Photo courtesy A & Z Pearls Inc.

Fig. 16.18 Photo courtesy Cultured Pearl Associations of America & Japan

Fig 17a Blue chalcedony and pearl necklace and earrings by Sandy Jones of Pearlworks. *Photo by Azad.*

Left: **Fig 17b** Brooch with pearls, rubellite raspberry, and leaf of liddicoatite tourmaline by Eve Alfillé. The raspberry is removable and may be worn as a pendant. *Photo by Matthew Arden.*

Below: **Fig 17c** Amethyst carved by Dieter Lorenz and South Sea pearl accented with diamonds. *Ring by Eve Alfillé; photo by Matthew Arden.*

17

Creating Unique Pearl Jewelry with Colored Gems

More and more designers are adding colored gems to their pearl jewelry. On the next few pages are some examples of how a variety of gems are being used to create innovative jewelry.

Fig. 17.1 Pin/clasp with carved black opal, green sapphires, freshwater pearls and Tahitian pearl drop on a necklace of cultured freshwater pearls and iolite beads. *Carving, design, fabrication & photo by Angela Conty.*

Fig. 17.2 Ruby & Japanese keshi necklace with matching ruby & Chinese freshwater pearl earrings designed by Sandy Jones, Pearlworks; photo by Azad.

Fig. 17.3 Wire-wrapped lavender spinel oval beads and pink Chinese freshwater pearl tassle. *Necklace by Sandy Jones, Pearlworks; photo by Azad.*

Fig. 17.4 Aquamarine and keshi-type freshwater cultured pearls (also called reborn pearls or Zai Sheng Zhu in Mandarain, see page 22). *Necklace from Yokoo Pearls Inc; photo from Inter World Trading.*

Fig 17.5 Tahitian and Australian South Sea cultured pearls strung with aquamarine, morganite and green beryl. *Necklaces from King Plutarco; photo by Richard Rubins.*

Fig. 17.6 Rutilated quartz crystal beads intertwined with dyed and natural-color freshwater pearls. The necklace can be worn with the strands twisted or draped. *Photo and necklace by Betty Sue King of King's Ransom.*

Fig. 17.7 Chinese freshwater pearls and tourmaline crystals. *Necklace, Eve Alfille; photo Matt Arden.*

Fig. 17.8 Japanese button-shaped freshwater pearls set in a matrix turquoise pin and accented with tourmalines. *Pin by Fred & Kate Pearce, photo by Tommy Elder.*

Test Your Gem IQ

In most cases you can't identify a gem just by looking at it, but you can make good guesses. Try to identify the gems in these designer pieces. The answers are below:

Fig. 1 Pearce Design. *Photo by Ralph Gabriner*

Fig. 2 Pearce Design. *Photo: R. Gabriner*

Fig. 3 Eve J. Alfillé. *Photo, Matthew Arden.*

Fig. 1 From top: Tahitian pearl strand, tsavorites, tanzanite, black opal, and American (Mississippi) freshwater pearl drop.

Fig. 2. From top: three 5mm cultured freshwater pearls, green tourmaline, five 3mm cultured freshwater pearls, chalcedony, dyed-black Akoya pearl.

Fig. 3. Left & right: three natural abalone pearls from the coast of Baja California and an irradiated pink diamond. From top: sapphire & pink sapphire cabochons, diamonds. The removable drop has a translucent aquamarine and a tanzanite briolette.

For more information on identifying colored gemstones, consult the *Gemstone Buying Guide: How to evaluate, identify, select & care for colored gems* by Renée Newman.

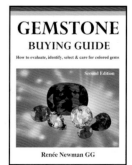

18

Caring for Your Pearls

Which of the following is hardest and which is softest?

♦ A pearl
♦ An opal
♦ Pure gold
♦ A tooth

The hardest is the opal. It has a hardness of 5 1/2–6 1/2 on the Moh's scale, which rates the relative hardness of materials from 1 to 10. (The 10 rating of a diamond is the highest, but a diamond is over 1000 times harder than an opal.) **Hardness** is a material's resistance to scratching and abrasions.

The softest of the four materials above is pure gold, which has a hardness of 2–2 1/2. When alloyed with other metals, the hardness of gold increases, but it is still a relatively soft metal.

Tooth enamel has a hardness of 5, and a pearl has a range of 2 1/2– 4. In other words, a pearl is a relatively soft material.

Knowing how soft a pearl is can help us understand why pearls should not be tossed on top of or next to other gems in a jewelry box. Knowing that a tooth is harder than a pearl helps us understand why the "tooth test" for identifying imitations should only be done very lightly or else avoided. The basic concept of hardness is that a harder material will scratch one that is softer.

Besides being soft, pearls are easily damaged by chemicals or eaten away by acids such as vinegar and lemon juice. Heat can turn pearls brown or dry them out and make them crack.

One advantage of pearls is they are fairly tough considering their softness. In his book *Pearls*, Alexander Farn relates how jewelers and pearl merchants of old would separate imitation pearls from real ones by having footmen stomp on them. Those that were crushed were imitation. The natural pearls normally would resist such blows. Cultured pearls, especially those with thin nacre, are not this durable. Therefore, avoid dropping or crushing them.

Cleaning Your Pearls

The softness of pearls and their low resistance to heat and chemicals mean that special precautions must be taken when cleaning them. Keep in mind the following guidelines:

♦ Do not use commercial jewelry cleaners on pearls unless the labels say they are safe for pearls. Many of them contain ammonia, which will cause deterioration.

♦ Never clean pearls in an ultrasonic cleaner. It can damage the pearls and wash out the color if the pearls have been dyed.

♦ Never steam-clean pearls. Heat can harm them.

♦ Never use detergents, bleaches, powdered cleansers, baking soda or ammonia-based cleaners on pearls.

♦ Do not use toothbrushes, scouring pads or abrasive materials to clean pearls. They can scratch their surface. If there's a lump of dirt that can't be rubbed off with a soft cloth, try using your fingernails. They have a hardness of only 2 1/2 or less.

Cleaning pearls is not complicated. After you wear them, just wipe them off with a soft cloth or chamois which can be dry or damp. This will prevent the dirt from accumulating and keep perspiration, which is slightly acidic, from eating away at the pearl nacre.

If the pearls have not been kept clean and are very dirty, they can be cleaned by your jeweler or they can be washed in water and a mild soap such as Ivory or Lux liquid (some liquid soaps, such as Dawn, can damage pearls) and cleaned with a soft cloth. Pay attention to the areas around the drill holes where dirt may tend to collect. After washing them, lay the pearls flat in a moist kitchen towel to dry. After the towel is dry, they should be dry. Do not wear pearls when their string is wet. Wet strings stretch and attract dirt which is hard to remove. Likewise do not hang pearls to dry.

Storing Your Pearls

Pearls are composed of about 2 to 4% water along with calcium carbonate and an organic binder called conchiolin. If the pearls become dehydrated, they can get brittle and crack. Consequently, they should not be kept near heaters or in places that get strong sunlight, such as on a window sill. Safe deposit boxes can be unusually dry, so if you ever store pearls there, try to take them out occasionally and expose them to humidity or moisture. Sealed plastic bags are not the best place for pearls. They can keep them from breathing and getting moisture.

Since pearls are soft, they should be kept in something that will protect them from scratches. Jewelry pouches or cloth bags are ideal. Pearls can also be wrapped in soft material and kept wherever convenient. Jewelry boxes may be handy, but they are also the first place burglars look.

Having Your Pearls Strung

Pearl necklaces can stretch with time and the string can get dirty and weak. Thus, they should be restrung periodically—about once a year, but that depends on how often they are worn. Fine pearls should be strung with silk and with knots tied between each pearl. This prevents them from rubbing against each other and from scattering if the string should break.

Occasionally pearls are strung with gold beads. According to a Los Angeles pearl stringer, gold turns pearls ivory-colored and coral black, and this is a permanent discoloration. Therefore, it's not advisable to string expensive pearls with gold beads.

Miscellaneous Tips

♦ Take your pearls off when applying cosmetics, hair sprays and perfume. These beauty aids are made of chemicals and acids which can harm your pearls.

♦ Take your pearls off when showering or swimming. It's not good to get the string wet, plus the chlorine or soap can damage the pearls. Pearl rings should be taken off when washing your hands or the dishes. Put the ring in a protective container or safe spot where it won't accidentally fall in the drain or get lost.

♦ When selecting pearl jewelry, check to see if the pearl is mounted securely. Preferably, the pearl will have been drilled and glued to a post on the mounting, especially if it is a ring. Otherwise, the pearl may come loose. If the pearl is flawless, a drill hole could lower its value. In such a case, it would be safer to set the undrilled pearl in a pin, pendant or earring than in a ring.

♦ When taking off a pearl ring, grasp the shank or metal part rather than the pearl. This will prevent the pearl from loosening and coming into contact with skin oil on your hand.

♦ Avoid wearing pearls with rough fabrics such as Shetland wool. They can scratch the pearls.

♦ About every six months, have a jewelry professional verify that the pearls on your jewelry are securely mounted or that the string is still good. Many jewelers will do this free of charge, and they'll be happy to answer your questions regarding the care of your jewelry.

19

Finding a Good Buy

Charlene is in a jewelry store. She's telling Scott, the owner, that she wants a nice pearl necklace but she's on a very limited budget. Although she's looked elsewhere, she hasn't found a strand she likes at a good price.

Scott first shows her a strand of Japanese saltwater pearls. He points out that the pearls are round and well matched, but their pearl coating is very thin. Consequently the strand is not a good choice for long-term, every-day wear. He adds that the round white saltwater pearls in her price range tend to have a thin coating, no matter where they're sold. Charlene wonders why no other jewelers ever mentioned this to her.

Scott then shows her some strands of freshwater pearls and asks her to compare them to the first strand. They're a lot more lustrous. Then he helps Charlene pick out an affordable strand that looks good on her. Charlene is impressed with Scott's selection of pearls and his straightforward approach. She plans on coming back to him for the rest of her jewelry needs, including a strand of good saltwater pearls when she has more to spend.

Matt wants to buy his wife some pearls for their 30th anniversary, since this is the traditional gift. He and his wife have been happily married for many years, so he wants the pearls to be of unusually fine quality. Matt has read The *Pearl Buying Guide* and is aware that pearls have many subtle quality differences. He realizes he will need some expert help.

As he shops, he discovers that he knows more than a lot of the salespeople. Eventually, Matt finds somebody who is really knowledgeable about pearls—Sandy, a college student who works part-time to pay her way through school. Sandy has always had a keen interest in gems, especially pearls, and she takes advantage of every opportunity to learn as much as possible about them.

Matt already knows that he wants either pink or white saltwater pearls in the 7 to 8 millimeter range. Sandy brings out a variety of strands and points out the fine nuances of luster, color and surface markings. Then she helps him choose two strands, which they will have strung with three mystery clasps. That way his wife can wear the pearls in different necklace lengths and as a bracelet. This is a quick and easy sale for Sandy, and it's a pleasant experience for Matt. He's gotten efficient, professional help and exactly the kind of pearls he was looking for.

Lisa is in a Tahitian jewelry store looking through a bowl of black pearls. Before coming to Tahiti on holiday, she read the *Pearl Buying Guide*. The salesman in the store tells her that she can have any of the pearls in the bowl for the equivalent of $120. Lisa first picks out the ones with the best luster. Then she eliminates those that are either too light or have no overtone colors. Finally, she ends up with a fairly large, tear-drop-shaped, dark-gray pearl with some greenish and purplish highlights. One side of the pearl, however, is badly flawed. But Lisa plans to wear it as a pendant, so the flaws won't show.

On the flight back home, she sketches a design for the pendant and then later has her jeweler make it. He tells her he could never find a black pearl as attractive as hers for such a low price. When the pendant is finished, Lisa tries it on. She's very pleased with how it looks. But she's even more pleased that she owns a unique piece which she has helped create.

Shopping for pearls turned out to be a positive experience for Lisa, Matt and Charlene. This was largely because they took the time to learn about pearls beforehand and/or they dealt with a competent salesperson. Listed below are some guidelines that helped them and can help you when you shop for pearls.

♦ **Look for luster.** This was the first quality factor that Lisa focused her attention on because it's the most important one. To understand why, just compare dull milky pearls to some highly lustrous ones. Chapter 4 gives you tips on judging luster.

♦ **When judging prices, try to compare pearls of the same type, shape, size, color, luster and blemish quality.** All of these factors affect the cost of pearls. Due to the complexity of pearl pricing, it' easier for consumers to compare pearls that are alike or at least similar.

♦ **Look at a variety of qualities** so you'll have a basis for comparison.

♦ **Remember that there is no standardized system for grading pearls.** As a consequence, grades such as "A" have no meaning other than what the seller assigns to them. In some cases, an "A" grade may be the lowest quality a store stocks. The lack of standardization does not mean there's no point in grading pearls. It's just an added reason why you need to know how to judge pearl quality yourself.

♦ **Be willing to compromise.** Both Charlene and Lisa had to settle for something other than what they might have preferred in order to stay within their budget. Charlene got freshwater instead of saltwater pearls. Lisa's pearl was badly flawed on one side. Even people with unlimited budgets have to compromise sometimes on the size, shape, color or quality due to lack of availability. A pearl doesn't have to be perfect for you to enjoy it.

♦ **Beware of sales ads that seem too good to be true.** The advertised pearls might be of unacceptable quality, especially in terms of nacre thickness. Or they might be stolen or misrepresented. Jewelers are in business to make money, not to lose it.

♦ **If possible, establish a relationship with a jeweler** you can trust and who looks after your interests. He can help you find buys you wouldn't find on your own.

♦ **Place the pearls against your hand and answer the following questions.** A negative answer suggests the pearls are a poor choice.

a. Do the pearls have bright, sharp light reflections?
b. Do the pearls have overtone colors? (This is a characteristic of pearls with good luster.)
c. Does the color of the pearls look good next to your skin?

The preceding guidelines in essence suggest that you learn how to evaluate pearls. But why is it so important for you to do this? Why should jewelers educate you about pearl quality? Is it just to help you compare prices?

No. Learning more about pearls will help you make a choice you can enjoy for a lifetime and will help you appreciate the unique qualities of the pearls you choose. How can you appreciate something you don't understand?

As you learn to compare luster differences among pearls, you will see how pearl brilliance differs from that of other gems. The brilliance of faceted gems normally appears best in their face-up position. No matter how you hold or wear good pearls, they glow. Even away from light they glow. And this glow has an intensity and depth unmatched by any other shiny round object.

As you learn to compare the color nuances of pearls, you'll see that good pearls are not just white. They have a variety of underlying colors which add to their beauty. And they come in a wide spectrum of body colors. Some people say that pearls make them look washed out. These people change their mind when they see black pearls and when they try on lighter pearls that enhance their body coloring.

As you are introduced to the different pearl shapes, you'll see how pearls offer creative design possibilities unlike any other gem. Even a basic strand of round pearls can be worn in creative, versatile ways.

Pearls can be worn anywhere, at any time, with anything. And even though pearls offer all these positive features, you don't have to be rich to own fine-quality pearls. If you are willing to compromise on the type of pearls you choose, you should be able to find good ones to fit almost any budget.

But to spot good pearls, you need to know how to judge their quality. So look at pearls whenever possible. Take time to analyze them. Ask jewelers to explain their quality differences. Gradually, you'll learn to recognize good value, and you'll see that the pearl is a remarkable gem which has no peer.

Suppliers of Pearls & Jewelry for Photographs

Cover photo: King Plutarco, Inc, Los Angeles, CA

Inside front cover photos: Eve J. Alfillé Gallery, Evanston, IL
  A & Z Pearls, Inc. Los Angeles, CA

Inside back cover photos: King Plutarco, Inc, Los Angeles, CA

Half-title page photo: A & Z Pearls, Inc, Los Angeles, CA

Photo facing title page: Hikari South Sea Pearl Co., Inc., Los Angeles, CA

Title page photo: Krespi & White Jewelry Inc., Oakland, CA

Chapter 1
Page 9   King Plutarco, Inc, Los Angeles, CA

Chapter 2
Figs. 2.2 - 2.4 Hikari South Sea Pearl Co., Inc., Los Angeles, CA

Chapter 3
Figs. 3.1 & 3.14   Hikari South Sea Pearl Co., Inc., Los Angeles, CA
Fig. 3.2   A & Z Pearls, Inc., Los Angeles, CA
Fig. 3.3   Overland Gems, Los Angeles, CA
Fig. 3.4   Erica Courtney, Hollywood, CA
Fig. 3.5   Albert Asher South Sea Pearl Co., Inc., New York, NY
Figs. 3.6, 3.7 & 3.10 King Plutarco Inc., Los Angeles, CA
Figs. 3.8, 3.9, 3.13 Eve J. Alfillé Gallery, Evanston, IL
Figs. 3.11 & 3.34   A & Z Pearls, Inc., Los Angeles, CA
Fig. 3.12 & 3.17 Pacific Coast Pearls, Petaluma, CA
Figs. 3.15 & 3.16 Inter World Trading, San Francisco, CA
Fig. 3.18 Art Jewelry, Charleston, SC
Fig. 3.19 Mikimoto (America) Ltd., New York, NY
Figs 3.20, 3.21 & 3.25, Pacific Coast Pearls, Petaluma, CA
Fig. 3.22 Blue River Gems & Jewelry, Fulton CA
Figs 3.23 & 3.24   Mikimoto (America), Ltd., New York, NY
Figs. 3.26, 3.27, 3.29, 3.30 Eve J. Allfilé Gallery
Fig. 3.28 KCB, San Francisco, CA
Fig. 3.31 Divina Pearls
Fig. 3.32   Mark Schneider Design, Long Beach, CA

Chapter 4
Figs. 4.1 & 4.2 Jye's International, Inc., San Francisco and Shima Pearl Co., Los Angeles, CA
Figs. 4.3 - 4.5 King Plutarco, Inc., Los Angeles, CA

Chapter 5
Figs. 5.1 - 5.3 King Plutarco, Inc., Los Angeles, CA
Fig. 5.9 King's Ransom, Sausalito, CA
Fig. 5.5 Shima Pearl, Co., Inc., Los Angeles, CA
Fig. 5.6 Josam Diamond Trading Corp., Los Angeles CA
Fig. 5.7 Assael International, Inc., New York, NY
Fig. 5.8 Shima Pearl Co., Inc., Los Angeles, CA
Fig. 5.10 Jye's International, Inc., San Francisco, CA

Chapter 8
Fig. 8.3 Albert Asher South Sea Pearl Co., Inc., New York, NY

Chapter 9
Fig. 9.1 Hikari South Sea Pearl Co., Inc., Los Angeles, CA
Fig. 9.2 King Plutarco, Inc., Los Angeles, CA
Fig. 9.3 Gary Dulac Goldsmith, Inc, Vero Beach, FL
Fig. 9.4 Erica Courtney, Hollywood, CA
Fig. 9.5 Krespi & White Jewelry Inc., Oakland, CA
Figs. 9.6 & 9.7 Albert Asher South Sea Pearl Co., Inc., New York, NY
Figs. 9.8 & 9.9 King Plutarco, Inc., Los Angeles, CA
Fig. 9.10 Albert Asher South Sea Pearl Co., Inc., New York, NY

Chapter 10
Fig. 10.1 Linda K. Quinn Designs, Strafford, MO
Fig. 10.2 Pacific Coast Pearls, Petaluma, CA
Fig. 10.3 Divina Pearls, Santa Monica, CA
Fig. 10.4 Eve J. Alfillé Gallery, Evanston, IL
Fig. 10.5 Assael International, Inc., New York, NY
Figs. 10.6 & 10.7 Erica Courtney, Hollywood, CA
Figs. 10.8 & 10.10 King Plutarco, Inc., Los Angeles, CA
Fig. 10.9 Erica Courtney, Hollywood, CA
Fig. 10.11 King Plutarco, Inc., Los Angeles, CA
Figs. 10.12 & 10.13 Mark Schneider Design, Long Beach, CA
Fig. 10.14 Ponthieux's Jewelry Design, Greenville, SC

Chapter 11
Figs. 11.1–11.3 A & Z Pearls Inc., Los Angeles, CA
Fig. 11.4–11.6 Pearce Design, West Lebanon, NH
Figs. 11.4 & 11.5 A & Z Pearls, Inc., Los Angeles, CA
Fig. 11.7 Eve J. Alfillé Gallery, Evanston, IL
Fig. 11.8 Linda K. Quinn Designs, Strafford, MO
Figs. 11.9 & 11.10, Pearlworks, Atlanta, GA
Fig. 11.11 A & Z Pearls, Inc., Los Angeles, CA
Figs. 11.12 & 11.15 Shogun Pearl, Harrison, NY
Figs 11.16 & 11.17, Pearce Design, West Lebanon, NH

Chapter 12
Fig. 12.3 King Plutarco, Inc., Los Angeles, CA
Fig. 12.7 Shima Pearl Co. Inc., Los Angeles, CA
Fig. 12.8 Erica Courtney, Hollywood, CA
Fig. 12.9 Shima Pearl Co., Inc., Los Angeles, CA
Fig. 12.10 Divina Pearls, Santa Monica, CA
Fig. 12.11 Angela Conty Designs, Schenectady, NY

Chapter 14
Figs. 14.1–14.3 K. C. Bell Natural Pearls, San Francisco, CA
Fig. 14.4 Eve J. Alfillé Gallery, Evanston, IL
Fig. 14.5 Angela Conty, Schenectady, NY
Fig. 14.8 Mikimoto (America) Ltd., New York, NY

Chapter 15
Fig. 15.1–15.4 Albert Cohen Co., Los Angeles, CA
Figs. 15.5 & 15.6 A & Z Pearls, Inc., Los Angeles, CA
Figs. 15.7 & 15.8 Inter World Trading, San Francisco, CA
Figs. 15.9–15.15, 15.18, 15.19, 15.21 Divina Pearls, Santa Monica, CA
Figs. 15.16 & 15.20 Shima Pearl Co., Inc., Los Angeles, CA

Chapter 16
Figs. 16a, 16b Divina Pearls, Santa Monica, CA
Figs. 16.1–16.15 & 16.17 A & Z Pearls Inc., Los Angeles, CA
Fig. 16.7 (The pearl shortener) Timeless Gem Designs, Los Angeles, CA
Fig. 16.14 (The mabe pearl enhancer) Shima Pearl Co., Inc., Los Angeles, CA

Chapter 17
Fig. 17.1 Angela Conty Designs, Schenectady, NY
Figs. 17.2 & 17.3 Sandy Jones, Pearlworks, Atlanta, GA
Fig. 17.4 Yokoo Pearls Inc. & Inter World Trading, San Francisco, CA
Fig. 17.5 King Plutarco, Inc., Los Angeles, CA
Fig. 17.6 King's Ransom, Sausalito, CA
Fig. 17.7 Eve J. Alfillé Gallery, Evanston, IL
Fig. 17.8 Pearce Design, West Lebanon, NH

Test Your Gem IQ
Figs. 1 & 2 Pearce Design, West Lebanon, NH
Fig. 3 Eve J. Alfillé Gallery, Evanston, IL
Gemstones on book cover, Cynthia Renée Co., Fallbrook, CA

Appendix

Chemical, Physical, & Optical Characteristics of Pearls

(The information below is mainly based on the following three sources:

Gems by Robert Webster
GIA Gem Reference Guide
GIA Colored Stones Course, Chapters 13 & 14 (1980 version)

Chemical composition:	$CaCO_3$ (most of it aragonite, the rest calcite) 82 to 92%
	H_2O 2 to 4%
	Conchiolin 4 to 14%
	Other about 0.4%
Mohs' hardness:	2 1/2 to 4
Specific gravity:	White natural saltwater pearls: 2.66–2.76 except for some Australian pearls whose density may be as high as 2.78
	Black natural saltwater pearls (Gulf of California): 2.61–2.69
	Natural freshwater pearls: 2.66–2.78
	Japanese Akoya cultured pearls: 2.72–2.78 or more
	Mantle-tissue nucleated cultured pearls: 2.67–2.70
Toughness:	Usually good, but variable. Old, dehydrated, or excessively bleached pearls are not as tough.
Cleavage:	None
Fracture:	Uneven
Streak:	White
Crystal character:	An aggregate composed mostly of tiny orthorhombic (pseudo-hexagonal) aragonite crystals and sometimes hexagonal calcite crystals. Conchiolin, an organic binding material, is noncrystalline.
Optic Character:	AGG, if not opaque (also listed as doubly refractive)
Refractive Index:	1.530–1.685
Birefringence:	.155

Dispersion:	None
Luster:	Dull to almost metallic. Fractures may look pearly to dull.
Phenomena:	Orient. Varies from almost none to very noticeable.
Pleochroism:	None
Chelsea-filter reaction:	None
Absorption spectra:	Varies greatly, not diagnostic
Ultraviolet fluorescence:	None to strong light blue, yellow, green, or pink under both LW and SW. Natural color black pearls—weak to moderate red to orangy red under LW.
Reaction to heat:	Pearls can burn, split, crack, or turn brown in excessive heat such as an open flame. Prolonged heat may cause dehydration, which may cause the nacre to crack.
Reaction to chemicals:	Attacked by all acids. Lotions, cosmetics, perspiration, and perfumes can also damage the nacre.
Stability to light:	Stable except for some dyed pearls.
Effect of irradiation:	Darkens color
Transparency to x-rays:	Semitransparent
X-ray fluorescence:	Natural saltwater pearls—inert except for a few white Australian pearls, which fluoresce faintly, cultured saltwater pearls—moderately strong to very weak greenish yellow depending on nacre thickness, freshwater pearls—moderate to strong yellowish white.
X-radiograph:	Cultured pearls usually show a clear separation between core and nacre, and their core normally looks lighter than the nacre coating. A mantle tissue nucleus will look like a very dark, irregularly shaped void. Natural pearls show a more or less concentric structure, and they tend to look the same tone throughout or get darker in the center.

Quizzes

Quiz (Chapters 2 and 3)

Select the correct answer

1. A mother-of-pearl bead is:
a. as valuable as a pearl
b. less valuable than a pearl
c. more valuable than a pearl
d. another name for a pearl

2. Which of the following types of pearls is most likely to be round?
a. A cultured South Sea pearl
b. A natural South Sea pearl
c. An Akoya pearl with very thin nacre
d. An Akoya pearl with very thick nacre

3. Mikimoto pearls:
a. come from a special kind of oyster trademarked by the Mikimoto company.
b. have more flaws than most pearls.
c. come in a range of qualities.
d. are natural pearls.

4. Baroque pearls:
a. originate from Europe.
b. have irregular shapes.
c. are freshwater pearls.
d. are those set in ornate mountings.

5. Mabe assembled pearls may come from:
a. The mabe oyster
b. The white South Sea pearl (silver-lip) oyster
c. The black pearl (black-lip) oyster
d. All of the above

6. Semi-cultured pearls:
a. are imitation pearls.
b. are half natural and half cultured.
c. have a cultivation period which is half as long as that of a cultured pearl.
d. grow in oysters which are bred in a laboratory.

7. High-quality keshi pearls are noted for their:
a. high luster
b. unique shapes
c. iridescence
d. all of the above

True or false?

8. When judging prices, consumers should try to compare pearls of the same shape and type.

9. Cultured pearls are imitation pearls grown by man in an oyster.

10. A pearl must be round to be valuable.

11. Freshwater pearls are those which are cultivated in non-polluted waters.

12. Valuable natural pearls have been found in North, South, and Central America.

13. Cultured round pearls were first produced and marketed in the early 1900's.

14. Natural pearls are produced by implanting shell beads in oysters which breed naturally.

15. Nacre is the pearly substance secreted around an irritant by an oyster or mussel.

Answers:

1. b
2. c
3. c
4. b
5. d
6. a
7   d
8. T
9. F   They are not imitation pearls.
10. F
11. F
12. T
13. T
14. F
15. T

Chapter 4 Quiz

1. A jeweler says his pearls are AAA quality. You should conclude:
a. The pearls are of high quality.
b. The pearls may be of any quality.
c. The pearls are not graded properly because the highest possible grade is A+.
d. The pearls have a high luster. Quality factors such as shape and color also need to be indicated.

2. A large percentage of the Akoya pearls sold today:
a. have a very high luster.
b. have thick or very thick nacre.
c. have thin or very thin nacre.
d. none of the above.

3. You have a written appraisal that states your pearl necklace has very thick nacre. You should assume:
a. Your pearls have a nacre thickness of exactly .5 mm or more on all the pearls
b. Your pearls have a nacre thickness of approximately .5 mm or more on all pearls.
c. Your pearls have a nacre thickness of approximately .5 mm or more on most pearls of the strand
d. Nothing if the appraiser has not defined his/her nacre-thickness grades somewhere on the appraisal.

4. Which type of lighting will make pearls look the most lustrous?
a. a bare 100-watt light bulb
b. candlelight
c. daylight on a rainy day
d. a fluorescent light covered with a translucent plastic shade

True or False?
5. Today, cultured pearls tend to have thicker nacre than they did in the 1950's.
6. When the judging luster of a strand, you should roll the pearls slightly on a flat, white surface.
7. If a cultured pearl is left in an Akoya oyster for at least three years, it will have a high luster.
8. Pearls with very low luster are easy to spot because they look more like white beads than pearls.
9. There's no point in paying $25 for a loupe when you can find brand new ones for $10.
10. If a pearl has thick nacre, it will have a high luster.

Answers:
1. b There's no standardized pearl grading system, so a jeweler can assign whatever meaning he wants to a grade. Even standardized grades such as those for diamonds are misused and inflated by some salespeople. Therefore it's best to base your judgement of a gem on what it looks like rather than on a grade assigned to it.
2. c
3. d The grading of nacre thickness is not standardized. "Very thick nacre" can have a variety of meanings depending on which appraiser or jeweler is using the term.
4. a
5. F
6. T
7. F Not necessarily. Improper cultivation techniques, disease, and pollution are a few of the factors that can lower the luster of a pearl even though it is left in an Akoya oyster for a long period of time.
8. T
9. F A $10 loupe will generally distort what it magnifies. A 10-power, fully corrected loupe is an ideal gem magnifier. Unfortunately, it will cost more than $10 brand new.
10. F Not necessarily. South Sea pearls usually have thicker nacre than Akoya pearls, yet their luster tends to be lower. The quality of the nacre is just as important as its thickness. A pearl with very thick nacre can have a very low luster.

Chapter 5 Quiz

Select the correct answer

1. Which of the following body colors is priced the highest for an Akoya pearl?

a. gold
b. light pink
c. cream
d. champagne

2. Which of the following overtone colors is usually the most valued on an Akoya pearl?

a. green
b. silver
c. gold
d. pink

3. You look in a drill hole of pearl and you see a dark pink line between the nacre and the bead nucleus, this means:

a. The pearl comes from the pink-lip oyster.
b. Nothing in particular. It's an inherent characteristic of pearls with pink overtones.
c. The pearl has been dyed.

4. When judging the color of pearls, you should examine them:

a. on a black background.
b. on a white background.
c. on a background the same color as their body color.
d. hanging in the air.

5. Which of the following can affect your perception of pearl color?

a. The color of the room you are in
b. The lighting
c. Alcoholic beverages
d. All of the above

Answers:

1. b

2. d

3. c

4. b

5. d

Chapter 6 Quiz

1   Which of the following is the least serious?
a.   missing nacre
b.   a crack
c.   a scratch
d.   a large discoloration

2.   Which of the following can affect the way you grade the flaws on a strand of pearls?
a.   The background the pearls are viewed against
b.   The lighting
c.   Your eyesight
d.   All of the above

3.   Which is the least serious?
a.   A bump next to a drill hole
b.   A visible discoloration on a single pearl
c.   A group of welts
d.   A cracked bead nucleus

4.   Flaws:
a.   Can help you prove that your pearls are real and not imitation.
b.   Can lower the price of pearls without affecting their overall beauty.
c.   Can help you distinguish your pearls from those of someone else.
d.   All of the above.

True or False?

5.   When checking for flaws on a strand, you should roll the pearls in order to see their entire surface.
6.   The longer a pearl is in an oyster, the more likely it is to have flaws.
7.   The term "pearl blemish" only refers to flaws that are on the surface of a pearl.
8.   Pearls with flaws are defective.

Answers:

1.   c
2.   d
3.   a
4.   d.
5.   T
6.   T
7.   F   It can also refer to internal flaws such as cracked nuclei and flaws that extend below the surface such as holes and missing nacre. The term "surface characteristic" can also mean internal flaw when it is applied to pearls.
8.   F   It's normal for pearls to have flaws.

Quiz (Chapters 7, 8 and 9)

1. Which would be the hardest to match?

a. Dyed Akoya pearls with very thick nacre
b. Dyed Akoya pearls with thin nacre
c. Non-dyed Akoya pearls with very thick nacre
d. Non-dyed Akoya pearls with thin nacre

2. Which would be the easiest to match?

a. 9 to 9 1/2 mm Akoya pearls
b. 9 to 9 1/2 mm South Sea pearls
c. 6 to 6 1/2 mm Akoya pearls
d. A graduated strand of South Sea pearls

3. Which of the following necklace lengths is shortest?

a. Opera
b. Matinee
c. Princess
d. Rope

4. Larger pearls can be cultivated in the South Seas than in Japan because:

a. the oysters in the South Seas are exposed to more sunlight.
b. South Sea oysters are larger than the Japanese Akoya type.
c. there are so many tropical fish for South Sea oysters to feed on.
d. none of the above

5. Which country has produced the most South Sea pearls and mother of pearl?

a. Burma
b. Australia
c. Japan
d. The Philippines

6. Which of these units of weight is heaviest?
a. 1 carat
b. 1 gram
c. 1 ounce avoirdupois
d. 1 pearl grain
e. 1 momme

7. Which of the following weighs the least?
a. 1 carat
b. 1 gram
c. 1 ounce avoirdupois
d. 1 pearl grain
e. 1 momme

True or False?

8. It's easier to match natural pearls than cultured pearls.
9. Mabe assembled pearls cost a lot less than South Sea pearls.
10. There's a regular rise in price as pearl size increases.
11. Two matched pearls can cost a lot more than two unmatched ones.
13. The effect of size on price can vary from dealer to another.

Answers:

1. c
2. c
3. c
4. b
5. b
6. c
7. d
8. F   It's a lot harder to match natural pearls.
9. T
10. F   Price jumps tend to be uneven.
11. T
12. F
13. T

Quiz (Chapters 10 and 12)

1. Which of the following is more valued on black pearls?

a. brown overtones
b. green overtones
c. gray overtones
d. no overtones

2. Which of the following is not used to darken the color of pearls?

a. Irradiation
b. Silver salt treatment
c. Heat treatment
d. Colored dyes

3. The size of most natural-color black pearls is usually:

a. less than 9 mm.
b. between 9 and 12 mm
c. between 11 and 15 mm
d. greater than 11.5 mm

4. A dyed-black pearl may have originally been:

a. an off-color Akoya pearl.
b. a light-color pearl from a black-lip oyster.
c. an off-color pearl from an Australian silver-lip oyster.
d. any of the above.

5. Which of the following shapes is the least expensive for a black pearl?

a. round
b. pear-shape
c. circled
d. oval

6. Today most natural-color black pearls are cultivated in:

a. Japan
b. Baja California
c. French Polynesia (Tahiti)
d. Australia

7. The term "black pearl" is used by jewelry salespeople to refer to:

a. natural-color black pearls from the black-lip oyster
b. "blue pearls"
c. dyed Akoya pearls
d. all of the above

True or False?

8. Most black pearls are very round.
9. Gray pearls are not considered to be black pearls.
10. Some cultured black pearls have an inadequate nacre coating.
11. If a pearl is black and over 11 mm in size, its color is natural.
12. Ring-like formations are often seen on Tahitian black pearls.
13. The most reliable way of determining if the color of a black pearl is natural is to have it x-rayed by a gem lab.
14. The color of "blue pearls" is stable.
15. There is no standardized system for classifying or valuing the color of black pearls.

Answers:
1. b
2. c
3. b
4. d   But if it's less than 8 mm, it was probably an off-color Akoya pearl.
5. c
6. c

7. d   Even though this book mainly uses the term "black pearl" to refer to natural-color pearls from the black-lip oyster, you should be aware that some people in the trade also use it to refer to any dark colored pearl, even "blue pearls" and dyed pearls. Therefore, always ask salespeople to specify what they mean by "black pearl."

8. F

9. F   Almost all black pearls are gray, not black.

10. T

11. F   Large pearls from the black-lip and silver-lip oysters are also dyed.

12. T

13. T

14. F   Due to their organic pigmentation, "blue pearls" can lose color or decay if holes are drilled through them. (See page 22 of *Pearls* by Shohei Shirai and the other references cited in the first section of this chapter.)

15. T

Chapter 11 Quiz

1. Most cultured freshwater pearls come from:
a. Japan
b. Korea
c. China
d. USA

2. Most freshwater pearls are:
a. round
b. semi-round
c. oval
d. baroque

3. The general term for any pearl cultivated in a lake, pond or river area is:
a. tissue-nucleated pearl.
b. natural sweetwater pearl
c. freshwater cultured pearl
d. b and c

4. What factor affects the price of freshwater pearls the least?
a. luster
b. smoothness
c. size
d. body color

5. What determines the shape of a pearl?
a. The type of nucleus inserted in the mollusk.
b. The position of the nucleus in the mollusk.
c. The length of time the pearl is in the mollusk.
d. All of the above.

True or False?
6. There is a wide difference of opinion as to what is the best color for a freshwater pearl.
7. The price of freshwater pearls is often quoted according to their weight in grams.
8. Iridescence and overtone colors are desirable characteristics for freshwater pearls.
9. High-quality freshwater pearls tend to cost more than high-quality saltwater pearls.

Answers:
1. c
2. d
3. c   Sweetwater pearl is another term for freshwater pearl, but if a pearl is cultivated in a pearl farm, it's not natural; it's cultured.
4. d
5. d.
6. T
7. T
8. T
9. F   Freshwater pearls tend to cost less.

Chapter 13 Quiz

1. A strand feels light in weight. There's a good chance it consists of:
a. Cultured pearls with thin nacre
b. Natural pearls
c. Plastic imitation pearls
d. Solid glass imitation pearls

2. Which of the following tests can prove that your pearls are not imitations?
a. The tooth test.
b. The surface magnification test
c. The overtone test
d. All of the above

3. Which is a typical characteristic of the drill holes of imitation pearls.
a. a clear dividing line between the coating and the core of the "pearl."
b. a straight hole with well defined edges
c. a thick coating of lacquer, paint, or pearl essence.
d. none of the above

4. Which of the following is an imitation pearl?
a. A semi-cultured pearl
b. A Majorica pearl
c. A faux pearl
d. b and c
e. a, b, and c

Pearl Buying Guide

5. Under 10-power magnification the surface of an imitation pearl tends to:
a. look grainy
b. show scaly maze-like patterns
c. appear striped
d. none of the above

6. If a jeweler can't tell that the pearls you are wearing are imitation or not this means:
a. He's a lousy jeweler.
b. He needs to read The *Pearl Buying Guide*.
c. He must have poor eyesight.
d. All of the above
e. None of the above.

Answers:

1. c
2. b   The results of the tooth and overtone tests are good indications but they don't provide positive proof. Some imitations feel gritty to the teeth and have overtones that vary. Thin-nacre pearls may have no overtones, and polished pearls may give a smooth tooth-test reaction.
3. d   The coating on imitation pearls tends to be very thin, not thick.
4. e   Majorica, faux, and semi-cultured pearls are all imitations.
5. a
6. e   Even pearl specialists can be fooled by imitations, particularly when viewing pearls from a distance. In some cases, they may need to examine the pearls under magnification to determine that they are imitation.

Chapter 14 Quiz

1. As you rotate a strand of "pearls" under a light, they blink and/or show faint stripes. This indicates the "pearls" are:
a. imitation   c. natural
b. cultured   d. Imitation or cultured

2. You are examining a "pearl." Its drill hole looks ragged and some of the coating has peeled off around it. This means the "pearl" is:
a. imitation.   c. either imitation or cultured
b. cultured.   d. either cultured or natural

3. Which of the following can help a gemologist distinguish between natural and cultured pearls?
a. An X-ray test   c. A hardness test
b. A refractometer test   d. All of the above

4. Natural pearls:
a. tend to be very round
b. tend to have greenish overtones
c. tend to have smaller drill holes than cultured pearls and imitations.
d. None of the above.

150

5. An appraiser tells you your pearls must be sent to another lab for an x-ray in order to determine if they are natural. The appraiser:
a. is not very competent.
b. has a poorly equipped lab.
c. is trying to make extra money on unnecessary lab tests.
d. is correct, and this does not mean that he/she is a poor appraiser.

True or False?
6. If an antique pearl piece was made before 1900, the pearls in it are natural.
7. Most cultured pearls tend to be slightly heavier than natural pearls.
8. Natural pearls tend to have irregular shapes.
9. The nacre of cultured pearls has a different chemical composition than that of natural pearls.

Answers:
1. d   Imitation pearls with shell cores and translucent coatings can show stripes like those of thin-nacre cultured pearls.
2. c.   The coating can peel off of both imitation and cultured pearls leaving their core exposed.
3. a
4. c
5. d
6. F   When natural pearls fall out of antique pieces, they are often replaced with cultured pearls or imitations.
7. T
8. T
9. F

Chapter 18 Quiz

True or False?
1. The best way to clean pearls is to put them in an ultrasonic cleaner.
2. You should take your pearls off when you shower or go swimming.
3. Decorative gold beads strung between pearls never damage or discolor the pearls.
4. The pearl is an ideal gem for an every-day wedding ring.
5. You should put on make-up and perfume before you put on your pearls.
6. Pearls should **not** be worn when their string is wet.
7. It doesn't matter if hair spray gets on your pearls because the lacquer makes them more lustrous and serves as a protective coating.
8. After wearing pearls, it's a good idea to wipe them off with a chamois.

Answers:
1. F   Pearls should never be placed in ultrasonic cleaners.
2. T,   3. F,   4. F,   5. T,   6. T,   7. F,   8. T

Bibliography

Books and Booklets

Ahrens, Joan & Malloy, Ruth. *Hong Kong Gems & Jewelry*. Hong Kong: Delta Dragon, 1986.

Anderson, B. W. *Gem Testing*. Verplanck, NY: Emerson Books, 1985.

Arem, Joel. *Gems & Jewelry*. New York: Bantam, 1986.

Bauer, Dr. Max. *Precious Stones*. Rutland, Vermont & Tokyo: Charles E. Tuttle, 1969.

Bingham, Anne. *Buying Jewelry*. New York: McGraw Hill, 1989.

Blakemore, Kenneth. *The Retail Jeweller's Guide*. London: Butterworths, 1988.

Bruton, Eric, *Legendary Gems or Gems that Made History*. Radnor, PA: Chilton 1986.

Ciprani, Curzio & Borelli, Alessandro. *Simon & Schuster's Guide to Gems and Precious Stones*. New York: Simon and Schuster, 1986.

Dickenson, Joan Younger. *The Book of Pearls*. New York: Crown Publisher's, 1968.

Farn, Alexander E. *Pearls: Natural, Cultured and Imitation*. London: Butterworths, 1986.

Farrington, Oliver Cummings. *Gems and Gem Minerals*. Chicago: A. W. Mumford, 1903.

Federman, David & Hammid, Tino. *Consumer Guide to Colored Gemstones*. Shawnee Mission: Modern Jeweler, 1989.

Freeman, Michael. *Light*. New York: Amphoto, 1988.

Gemological Institute of America. *Gem Reference Guide*. Santa Monica, CA: GIA, 1988.
Gemological Institute of America. *The GIA Jeweler's Manual*. Santa Monica, CA: GIA, 1989.
Gemological Institute of America. *Proceedings of the International Gemological Symposium* 1991. GIA, 1992.

Greenbaum, Walter W. *The Gemstone Identifier*. New York: Prentice Hall Press, 1988.

Hall, Cally, *Gemstones*, Eyewitness Handbooks. London: Dorling Kindersley, 1994.

Idaka, Kimiko. *Pearls of the World*. Tokyo: Shinsoshoku Co., 1985.

Jackson, Carole. *Color Me Beautiful*. New York: Ballantine, 1985.

Japan Pearl Exporters' Association. *Cultured Pearls*. Japan Pearl Exporters' Association.

Jewelers of America. *The Gemstone Enhancement Manual*. New York: Jewelers of America, 1990.

Joyce, Kristin & Addison Shellei. *Pearls: Ornament & Obsession*. New York: Simon & Schuster, 1993.

Kunz, George Frederick. *The Curious Lore of Precious Stones*. New York: Bell, 1989.

Kunz, George & Stephenson, Charles. *The Book of the Pearl*. New York: Century Co., 1908.

Landman, Neil; Mikkelsen, Pula; Bieler, Rudiger; Bronson, Bennet. *Pearls: A Natural History*. New York: Harry N. Abrams, 2001.

Liddicoat, Richard T. *Handbook of Gem Identification*. Santa Monica, CA: GIA, 1993.

Lintilhac, Jean-Paul. *Black Pearls of Tahiti*. Papeete, Tahiti: Royal Tahitian Pearl Book, 1985.

Matlins, Antoinette L. & Bonanno, A. *The Pearl Book*. South Woodstock, VT: Gemstone Press, 2002.

Marcum, David. *Fine Gems and Jewelry*. Homewood, IL: Dow Jones-Irwin, 1986.

Miguel, Jorge. *Jewelry, How to Create Your Image*. Dallas: Taylor Publishing, 1986.

Miller, Anna M. *Gems and Jewelry Appraising*. New York: Van Nostrand Reinhold Company, 1988.

Muller, Andy. *Pearls*. Kobe: Golay Buchel Japan, 1990.

Muller, Andy. *Cultured Pearls, the First Hundred Years*. Golay Buchel, 1997.

Nadelhoffer, Hans. *Cartier Jewels Extraordinary*. *New York: Harry Abrams, 1984.*

Nassau, Kurt. Gemstone Enhancement, Second Edition. London: Butterworths, 1994.

O'Donoghue, *Identifying Man-made Gems*. London: N.A.G. Press, 1983.

O'Donoghue, Michael & Joyner, Louise, *Identification of Gemstones*. Oxford: Butterworth-Heinemann, 2003

Powley, Tammy. *Making Designer Gemstone & Pearl Jewelry*. Glouster, MA: Rockport Publishers, 2003.

Preston, William S. *Guides for the Jewelry Industry*. New York: Jewelers Vigilance Committee, Inc., 1986.

Rosenthal, Leonard. *The Pearl and I*. New York: Vantage Press, 1955.
Rosenthal, Leonard. *The Pearl Hunter*. New York: Henry Schuman, 1952.

Salomon, Paule. *The Magic of the Black Pearl*. Papeete, Tahiti: Tahiti Perles, 1986.

Schumann, Walter. *Gemstones of the World*. New York: Sterling, 1997.

Shirai, Shohei. *Pearls*. Okinawa, Marine Planning Co. Ltd., 1981.

Smith, G.F. Herbert. *Gemstones*. London: Pitman, 1949.

Taburiaux, Jean. *Pearls: Their origin, treatment & identification*. Radnor, PA: Chilton, 1985.

Ward, Fred. *Pearls*. Bethesda, MD: Gem Book Publishers, 2002.

Webster, Robert. *Gemmologists' Compendium*. New York: Van Nostrand Reinhold, 1979.
Webster, Robert. *Gems*. London: Butterworths, 1983.
Webster, Robert. *Practical Gemmology*. Ipswich, Suffolk: N. A. G. Press, 1976.

Periodicals

Auction Market Resource for Gems & Jewelry. P. O. Box 7683 Rego Park, NY. 11374.

Australian Gemmologist. Brisbane: Gemmological Association of Australia

Canadian Gemmologist. Toronto: Canadian Gemmological Association.

Colored Stone. Devon, PA: *Lapidary Journal* Inc.

Gems and Gemology. Santa Monica, CA: Gemological Institute of America.

The Guide. Chicago: Gemworld International, Inc.

Lapidary Journal. Devon, PA: *Lapidary Journal* Inc.

Jewelers Circular Keystone. Radnor, PA: Chilton Publishing Co.

Jewelers' Quarterly Magazine. Sonoma, CA.

Journal of Gemmology, London: Gemmological Association and Gem Testing Laboratory of Great Britain.

Modern Jeweler. Lincolnshire, IL: Vance Publishing Inc.

National Jeweler. New York: Gralla Publications.

Palmieri's Auction/FMV Monitor. Pittsburgh, PA: GAA

Pearl World. Phoenix, AZ. Haggis House, Inc.

Rock & Gem. Ventura, CA: Miller Magazines, Inc.

Miscellaneous: Courses, Leaflets, etc..

A & Z Pearls Price List. Los Angeles, CA

"Cultured Pearls." The American Gem Society.

Gemological Institute of America Gem Identification Course. Santa Monica, CA.

Gemological Institute of America Colored Stones Course, 2002.

Gemological Institute of America Pearls Course, 1990.

"Grading and Information Guide." Midwest Gem Lab. Brookfield, Wi.

"Hints to select your cultured pearls." Rio Pearl. Hong Kong.

"I am a pearl." Mastoloni Pearls. New York, NY.

"Mastering Cultured Pearls." Adachi America Corporation. Los Angeles, CA.

"Pearl: Miracle of the Sea." American Gem Society.

"Pearl World." The International Pearling Journal. Haggis House, Inc., Phoenix, AZ., April to November 1993.

"Pearls of Japan." Japan Pearl Exporters' Association.

"Perle Noire: Quality comes first." Tahiti perles S C. Tahiti.

"Quality Cultured Pearls Price List." Adachi America. Los Angeles, CA.

"A Selling Guide for Retailers." Japan Pearl Exporters' Association.

"A Shopper's Guide to Cultured Pearls." J. C. Penney.

Shogun Trading Co. Price List. New York, NY.

Tara & Sons Inc. Price List. New York, NY

"Treasures from the Sea." Shogun Cultured Pearls. New York, NY.

"What you should know about cultured pearls." Jewelers' of America.

Index

OTHER BOOKS BY RENÉE NEWMAN

Diamond Handbook
How to Look at Diamonds & Avoid Ripoffs

Provides additional details and photos on cut & clarity, and covers topics not included in the *Diamond Ring Buying Guide* such as:
◆ Antique diamonds and jewelry
◆ Branded diamonds
◆ Diamond certificates, reports & appraisals
◆ Diamond recutting
◆ Diamond types
◆ Choosing a jeweler
◆ Using fluorescence to detect HPHT & CVD lab-grown diamonds

Some chapter headings and sub headings are:
◆ How do appraisers determine the retail replacement cost?
◆ What's the biggest disadvantage of synthetic gems?
◆ Pricing antique diamonds
◆ Getting your diamonds recut
◆ How to find a qualified independent appraiser
◆ What causes diamond fluorescence?
◆ How do cutters modify diamond color?
◆ Does a diamond report reveal everything you need to know?
◆ How reproducible are lab grades?

NEW
FOR 2005

186 pages, 7 color and 242 b/w photos, 6" x 9", ISBN 0-929975-36-7, $18.95 US

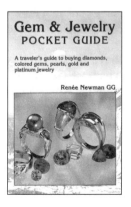

Gem & Jewelry Pocket Guide

"Brilliantly planned, painstakingly researched, and beautifully produced . . . this handy little book comes closer to covering all of the important bases than any similar guides have managed to do. From good descriptions of the most popular gem materials (plus gold and platinum), to jewelry craftsmanship, treatments, gem sources, appraisals, documentation, and even information about U.S. customs for foreign travelers—it is all here. I heartily endorse this wonderful pocket guide."

John S. White, former Curator of Gems & Minerals at the Smithsonian, *Lapidary Journal*

"Short guides don't come better than this. . . . As always with this author, the presentation is immaculate and each opening displays high-class pictures of gemstones and jewellery."

Journal of Gemmology

156 pages, 108 color photos, 4½" x 7", ISBN 0-929975-30-8, $11.95 US

Available at bookstores, jewelry supply stores or by mail

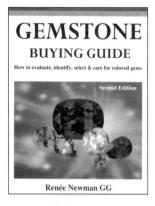

Gemstone Buying Guide
How to Evaluate, Identify and Select Colored Gems

"**Praiseworthy**, a beautiful gem-pictorial reference and a help to everyone in viewing colored stones as a gemologist or gem dealer would . . . one of the finest collections of gem photographs I've ever seen. . . . If you see the book, you will probably purchase it on the spot."

Anglic Gemcutter

"**A quality Buying Guide** that is recommended for purchase to consumers, gemmologists and students of gemmology—irrespective of their standard of knowledge of gemmology. The information is comprehensive, factual, and well presented. Particularly noteworthy in this book are the quality colour photographs that have been carefully chosen to illustrate the text."

Australian Gemmologist

"**Beautifully produced** . . . With colour on almost every opening few could resist this book whether or not they were in the gem and jewellery trade.

Journal of Gemmology

156 pages, 281 color photos, 7" x 9", ISBN 0-929975-34-0, $19.95 US

Ruby, Sapphire & Emerald Buying Guide
How to Evaluate, Identify, Select & Care for these Gemstones

"**Solid, informative and comprehensive** . . . dissects each aspect of ruby and sapphire value in detail . . . a wealth of grading information . . . a definite thumbs-up.

C. R. Beesley, President, American Gemological Laboratories
Jewelers' Circular Keystone

"**The best produced book on gemstones I have yet seen in this price range**. This is the book for anyone who buys, sells or studies gemstones. This style of book (and similar ones by the same author) is the only one I know which introduces actual trade conditions and successfully combines a good deal of gemmology with them. . . . **Buy it, read it, keep it**."

Michael O'Donoghue, *Journal of Gemmology*

An up-to-date, illustrated, reliable guide on how to purchase a ruby, sapphire or emerald. Of particular value are chapters devoted to the assessment of colour and clarity, value enhancing treatments, synthetics and imitations...and the desirable features of star ruby and sapphire. . . . The accuracy and clarity of this guide's information sets a standard to be emulated. "

Australian Gemmologist

164 pages, 178 color & 21 b/w photos, 7" x 9", ISBN 0-929975-33-2, $19.95 US

Available at bookstores, jewelry supply stores or by mail